NARCISSISTS

Step By Step Guide To Dealing With
Narcissism In Your Relationship, In Family
And At Your Workplace

John Stam

Contents

INTRODUCTION

Arrogance, pride, admiration and ego, are all acceptable emotions when exhibited in moderation. However, A narcissist, on the other hand, is arrogant, egotistical, and believes that they are entitled to whatever they want. So, what is narcissism exactly?

Narcissus, a young man who fell in love with a water pool reflection of himself, is the originator of narcissism in Greek mythology. Narcissus was a Boeotian Greek hunter. He was the son of a nymph and a river god. He was incredibly attractive. Narcissus was lured to the edge of a lake by Nemesis, who was so engrossed in admiring his reflection that he drowned. In today's world, narcissism is a psychoanalytic theory; the ideas find their origins in Sigmund Freud's book on narcissism. Narcissism is also classified as a psychiatric illness by the American Psychiatrist Association.

Narcissism is a form of personality disorder. The majority of psychologists and psychoanalysis experts believe that narcissism is a growing cultural and social issue. There is such a thing as healthy narcissism, which most psychologists refer to as a manifestation of healthy self-love. Most psychoanalysts believe, nevertheless, that the distinction between healthy self-love and narcissistic tendencies is razor-thin. That healthy self-love may quickly morph into narcissism without a person's awareness. Obsessing excessively over one's physical image may become a diversion from everyday life and activities.

In reality, along with Machiavellianism and Psychopathy, a narcissism personality disorder is one of the three dark personalities or the dark triad. The term "dark triad" was coined because these three diseases are all thought to have evil characteristics.

However, narcissism should not be confused with egocentrism. Certainly, narcissists and egocentrics are still overflowing with vanity, but there is a distinction to be made. When it comes from anyone else, narcissists get their fix of admiration or whatever supply they need at the time.

It's difficult to deal with narcissism, particularly when those who suffer from it don't see it as an issue. In reality, people with narcissism believe that they are perfectly good and natural. If anything or anything causes them to question how they live their lives, they will do their utmost to obscure the real facts that appear to them as attacks and get on with their lives.

Also, don't try to persuade them or even point out the issue, or you'll be in for a major, possibly bloody battle. In this book, we will look through some methods for overcoming narcissism or dealing with narcissistic attitudes at the workplace, in relationships and family life. The subsequent chapters will expound more on how narcissism affects us at all levels and the various applicable tips to help you understand and manage people with narcissistic attitudes.

CHAPTER ONE
NARCISSISTIC PERSONALITY DISORDER

A narcissist has a personality disorder in which they are obsessed with superiority, wealth, reputation, and vanity. They are blissfully unaware of the havoc they are wreaking on themselves and others. A so-called narcissist is capable of acting without regard for the feelings of those around them. They believe they are truly superior, and they demand respect. You may call them narcissistic or selfish; these are only a few of the labels that many people apply to narcissists. They are emotionally involved, and it is only natural for them to be hurt. They created this narcissistic version of themselves for it to act as a shock absorber.

Narcissistic pain, on the other hand, is distinct from other forms of emotional distress. People with narcissism often exhibit snobbish, patronizing, or even disdainful attitudes. He or she may, for example, complain about a bartender's rudeness or incompetence or end a medical examination with a dismissive assessment of the physician.

A personality disorder is a pattern of behavior that differs from that of the average person. Cognition, interpersonal functioning, impulse control, and effect are all examples of this pattern. The persistent trend isn't quite adaptable, and it can be seen in early childhood characteristics. The pattern is consistent and has lasted a long time.

Males are more prone to narcissism than females. However, as time passes and they suppress all of their emotions, this condition fades, and symptoms diminish in people in their 40s and 50s. An individual may become a narcissist for a variety of reasons. Today's researchers aren't sure what triggers an individual to become a narcissist in the first place. However, there are several hypotheses regarding the potential causes of narcissistic personality disorder.

The majority of practitioners believe in a bio-psychosocial model of causation, which states that the cause is most likely due to biological and genetic causes, as well as social factors such as how people interact with one another from childhood to the present. Consider psychological factors, such as a person's personality and temperaments influenced by their environment, as well as acquired coping skills for dealing with stress. This indicates that no single factor causes a person to become a narcissist; rather, the nuanced and possibly interconnected existence of all factors is crucial. It is suggested that if a person has this personality disorder, they become carriers and pass it on to their unknowing children.

This personality disorder may be treated, though it usually entails long-term psychotherapy or counselling with a psychiatrist who has extensive experience treating this type of personality disorder. Certain drugs can help with certain symptoms. This type of person exaggerates things around him, and they also have a habit of daydreaming about delusions of appearance, achievement, and power overpowering their thoughts. This person is also overly sensitive. They must be admired at all times in everything they do. They will be deeply hurt if they do not.

They also tend to exploit and take advantage of those around them by using their emotional emotions as a tool, which those around them must understand. They lack empathy, which allows us to sense and understand the needs of others. These are the envious people, and their actions come across as haughty or arrogant to us.

Untreated Narcissistic Personality Disorder increases the risk of substance misuse, including narcotics and alcohol, depression, relationship issues, job or school challenges, and suicidal activities or feelings. According to recent research, males with narcissism have higher cortisol levels in their blood. Since cortisol is a stress hormone, this condition is caused by too many stress-induced childhood experiences until they can no longer handle it.

And those who are not under a lot of stress have higher cortisol levels. Cortisol levels above a certain threshold have been related to an increased risk of heart disease. Family members of anyone suffering from this illness classify the sufferer as controlling and perpetually unhappy with what others do. The narcissist would never stop blaming others and making them feel responsible for their issues and current activities. They are characterized as being short and irritable. They lose their cool at the slightest provocation and believe that something is going against them. They would believe that everyone around them is constantly turning their backs on them and treating them silently.

In the worst-case scenarios, a person may become physically and sexually abusive. Living with a narcissist can feel like you're trapped in a nightmare. It's as if you've been arrested and have no means of getting out. Spouses, coworkers, bosses, and even parents may become trapped in relationships that are difficult to leave. The emotional and physical harm that a person with the condition may cause can be serious. Emotional fatigue affects all, including health care workers.

Narcissists use a facade and carefully created blind holes in their thinking to protect their fragile self-esteem. They live in a dream world where all of their needs are met and unreasonable expectations replace a life. They feel superior with this fantastical world they've concocted in their minds, oblivious to the impact they're having on those around them. They become obsessed with beauty and material possessions, as well as developing a superficial interest in things that aren't real, such as soap operas, movies, video games, and rock stars.

They are afraid of their emotions. They are unable to form and maintain deep friendships or intimate relationships, as well as establish mature love relationships. For a narcissist, a fantasy world can be a sweet diversion, but it can also become an attempt to avoid seeing what is there to boost self-esteem. To compensate for their secret broken childhood, narcissists process knowledge, emotions, and unresolved pain. They enjoy doing something in their created world through their imaginations, and they often make unreasonable demands on others to make themselves feel better. They aren't good at dealing with negative emotional distress, so they don't accept it. Instead of looking closely to see their part of the issue, they normally blame it on others. This is the projection defence: when a person does not like himself, he or she becomes enraged at others who share any of his or her likeable characteristics.

In a narcissistic perspective, the self-image is skewed, and the individual assumes that he is superior to others. An exaggerated sense of self-worth serves as a shield to hide the unforgivable guilt that lurks underneath the surface. Grandiosity is an insidious mistake that people make because they believe it is a preventative measure that keeps them from blaming themselves and being depressed or disintegrated.

The tone of their voice appeals to narcissists. They are people who thrive on being the centre of attention and who prefer to bring others down who they believe are inferior. A narcissist at work is power-hungry and would go to any extent to achieve it. Finding out if you're with a narcissist can be challenging and confusing, particularly if you're unsure about how you feel about the narcissist you're with.

Narcissists tend to work according to their laws. Since narcissists are just concerned about themselves, keep in mind that they will never make a good friend. They will befriend you to transform you into one of their victims or supply outlets. They will do favours for you in exchange for a large reward, and you will do the same for them. Unfortunately, you can't just do anything you want to this person at work and walk away without repercussions. So the safest course of action is to join him or her. Keeping in contact with a narcissist regularly will prevent them from assuming you dislike them. However, avoid getting too close to a narcissist because they think and process information differently than you do. Narcissists expect you to react immediately when they demand your attention, just like a regular boss in your workplace expects you to obey him in whatever he requests.

It's a no-no to share your thoughts with a narcissist because you're asking them to prioritize your feelings. Focusing on solutions rather than the problem is the next best thing you can do. The narcissist enjoys focusing on an issue and turning it over, around, rearranging it, and dissecting it. They tend to complicate things. Stop staring at the bottle as if it were half full. The only thing you can do is turn the situation around and persuade the narcissist to see the other side of the facts.

It's probably a good idea to just present a few options. The narcissist craves power, and if you have the opportunity to provide them with choices, they will adore you. This is one of the ways to make them feel as though you value their thoughts and are challenging them to take command and show you what they're made of. If it all doesn't work out, the best last resort is to make them feel good about themselves, special, and unique. Narcissists enjoy being admired and having the impression that they are superior to others. Being in control gives them a rush, and they thrive on praise and appreciation. Simply tell them how wonderful they are if you want them to be happy and prosperous for you. They feel at ease when you praise them.

When a narcissist is young, they develop the delusional illusion that the person they choose as a partner will provide them with true love and compensate for all of their life's hurts and slights. This burning need for unconditional love stems from an unmet need from their tumultuous childhood. Although most adults appreciate the benefits of unconditional love, they still recognize that it is an uncommon occurrence. This is because the people we love normally keep us accountable for our decisions in some way. Consider if you want to impose your neediness and bad conduct on others.

Being a narcissist is not easy, and those who suffer from this condition should not be dismissed or taken for granted. They assume all is perfect because that is how they grew up, and that is a normal occurrence for them. People with this type of condition need extra care and understanding; no one wants to be born with it. People who act narcissistically have a sense of entitlement that encourages them to disregard social laws. They assume that the law should not extend to them and that they will not be punished if they are captured. They are, however, dissatisfied with any inconveniences they have experienced as a result of being busted. They assume they have the right to do whatever they want to obtain immediate gratification without suffering any consequences.

Narcissism in the Real World

We've established what narcissism is, but what does it mean in daily life? Let's take a look at Raymond, a fictional character, to understand narcissism better.

Raymond is the district manager of a cooperative. He seems to be a diamond at first glance. He has all the qualities you'd expect from someone in his position: sweet, charming, and endearing. However, when you get to know Raymond better, you begin to notice some items that may or may not seem charming. When you contradict Raymond in sessions, whether at work or in social environments, he gets irritated. He isn't as receptive to suggestions as you might think. He considers his views to be extremely important, and as a result, he openly expresses them without regard for others. He will inquire about your thoughts, but it is merely a formality at this point and not something to which he can devote his time. He despises obstacles, is unaware of his ability to succeed, and despises criticism. He behaves as if he is a deity who needs to be worshipped. He needs his words to be taken seriously as gospel, and there is no disputing that.

He will exaggerate things if he is kept waiting or if things do not go his way. It is simple for such an individual to throw tantrums or engage in extremely undesirable behaviour. He would hold grudges against those who stand up to him, whether or not they are right. This is childish behavior, and it is not the only childish behavior he can display. He is the one who must get the table he needs at the snap of a finger as a man who is used to getting his way. When he doesn't get the table or the service he needs, he loses his cool quickly.

Raymond has no true friends as a result of these circumstances. His bloated ego and sense of importance gradually drive almost all of his friends away from him. While he has a downright charming demeanor and a generally gentlemanly demeanor, when you get to know him better, it all begins to crumble. Anyone who spends time with him gradually grows tired of his godlike, self-centred demeanor. He has trouble engaging with others and being attentive to their needs or desires because of his self-centeredness. Don't get me wrong: Raymond does support a few others, but only when it benefits him or advances his personal goals. It's also debatable whether Raymond considers himself to be friends with someone. In his opinion, he owes a few favors to a few people. People are tools to him, not mates. He employs them to carry out his wishes.

There is no distinction between Raymond and his self-righteousness. As a result, his wife, children, and neighbors find it difficult to connect and live with him because he wants others to agree with his viewpoints. Raymond is a narcissist in every sense of the word. And persuading him to admit it would be a difficult challenge. I'm not implying that Raymond is a bad guy. He may have a skewed sense of self-righteousness that seems correct to him but is severely distorted by a different viewpoint. He will never know it because his own viewpoint is the only one he is willing to consider. If his wife is not a quiet woman, he is very likely to argue with her often about trivial matters. It may be more difficult for such a person to maintain a family life than normal people. As a father, he will have a one-sided relationship with his children.

As I previously said, narcissism can be healthy in moderation. Confidence and firm belief in one's ability may be mistaken for narcissism. Esteem or arrogance may be mistaken for narcissism, but it is rarely a narcissistic characteristic. Many people in the world are self-assured; they trust in themselves and their abilities. Absolute confidence in one's ability is not the same as narcissism. The main distinction between these individuals and a narcissistic narcissist being that, unlike the narcissist, they do not regard themselves as superior to anyone (better than anyone) or claim special care. They don't insist on being treated differently because they are better than their peers. They devote more time and effort to the work or mission at hand. A self-assured, strong-willed person is more likely to succeed than a narcissist. While a narcissist spends his time admiring himself, the self-assured individual gets the job done.

This is not to say that they do not believe they are the best in their profession; rather, they are not envious of or hold grudges against other experienced people in their field of research. They are conscious of their own needs and feelings, as well as the needs and feelings of those around them. They don't believe that any chance to support someone else is an opportunity to further their own goals. They care for the people around them. The narcissist, on the other hand, is the polar opposite. He searches for shortcuts and ways to manipulate any situation to his advantage, regardless of the consequences for those around him. Jealousy and peer competition can also drive him to bring others he admires down. A narcissist can also fail to assist a colleague who works in the same sector as him. All because you despise that guy!

Here are some of the most common traits of a pathological narcissist.

1. They have a sense of entitlement as if all were theirs to have.
2. They are perpetual attention seekers who crave respect the majority of the time.
3. They are opportunistic. They will take advantage of a child if it helps them achieve their selfish goals.
4. If the pain or distress does not further his or her agenda, it is unimportant to them. They are unable to associate with any emotion or feeling that is not conducive to achieving their goals.
5. Their middle name is Jealousy. When anyone else wins the award instead of him or her, he or she will be envious and feel cheated.
6. They are deeply conceited.
7. They are preoccupied with fantasies of grandeur, untold wealth, elegance, perfect love, and marriage. They consider themselves to be on par with Albert Einstein in terms of genius.

CHAPTER TWO
IDENTIFYING THE COMMON TRAITS AND CHARACTERISTICS OF NARCISSISTS

Many markers can be used to classify a narcissist, but this does not mean that anyone who exhibits these behaviours is a narcissist. Remember that narcissism is a psychological disorder, and as such, other psychological disorders can manifest in the same ways that a narcissist does. The traits we'll look at will help you better understand a narcissist's mind, which can be quite useful when coping with anyone who has the disorder.

Fear of Being Rejected

The majority of narcissists have experienced mental distress. He is afraid of being rejected. In reality, this is the one thing he fears more than anything else in the world. He or she is acutely aware of something that he (for all intents and purposes, he refers to the narcissist) perceives as signs of imminent rejection. He considers rejection to be a humiliating experience reserved for the poor. He constructs a barrier around himself and refuses to let anyone near him. He assumes that if he places too much trust in others, he will be rejected or disappointed. He places a higher priority on material objects such as money than on relationships, and he is simply more in love with things than with people. To defend himself and prevent people from seeing the insecure person he considers himself to be, he will steal, deceive, and lie. He creates a facade and convinces himself that it is genuine, refusing to see the world through his filter. With his self-proclaimed sense of worth, he can't understand why anyone like him should ever have to hear "no." If he was raised as a spoiled brat, he is used to getting his way all of the time and becomes depressed and anxious when things don't go his way.

Develop a False self

We've seen how a child raised in society considers a natural, stable home environment matures into his true self. On the other hand, a child raised in an abusive home would not have this opportunity. He spent his whole childhood trying to fit into other people's shoes and never bothered to find his own. Every possible narcissist creates a false identity or self, whether it's an overachieving child who is always trying to please his parents or a rowdy teenager who goes out of his way to disappoint his relatives. They can also become slightly schizophrenic at times, with the potential to fully grow into multiple personalities later. He believes that the only one capable of fully appreciating him is himself.

It's not shocking that he talks to his other self or imaginary friend for most of his issues. In this way, he often justifies looking at an issue from various perspectives. As a result, he grows up unaware of his true identity. He creates a false self, and he is unwilling to communicate intimately with someone because he is searching for what he perceives to be perfect love. Love and affection may smack him in the face, but he may miss it because he is always on the lookout for the extraordinary. This is mostly due to his apprehensions of betrayal, rejection, and abandonment. He keeps a safe distance from everyone and does not allow anyone to get too close to him.

Furthermore, no one can get close enough to develop a meaningful relationship with him because he doesn't really know himself and hides behind his fake self. People who get close enough are hurt and sent away so that they won't consider rekindling the relationship. Furthermore, he is capable of one selfless act, "an act aimed at himself," because of his entitlement, which is similar to the Greek mythology of Narcissus.

Have a Narcissistic Circle

He would have a circle because he wants to be around people who he believes worship or support him. Consider the most famous high school student. He'll almost certainly have his own group of fans who hang out with him all the time. Either out of deference or to avoid being picked on. The narcissistic circle resembles the narcissistic circle in appearance. This group of people continually reminds the narcissist that he is the best thing that has ever happened to the planet. They just add to his already smouldering ego. Narcissist supply is a group of people who make up this circle.

The term "narcissist supply" refers to a group of people who give the narcissist the approval, attention, and appreciation he seeks. The narcissist's false self needs this supply source and considers it essential to his survival. The narcissist's ego inflates like an air balloon due to this relentless barrage of admiration, whether fake or genuine. To keep his ego fed, he relies on a steady stream of admiration and attention. He starts to depend on this circle more than he would like to admit, unbeknownst to himself. When we look at the big picture, it reminds us of the bully and his gang of cowards who depend on the bigger kid for safety and laugh at every joke he tells.

The narcissistic supply circle is no better than the narcissist, and since the narcissist is eager to rise to the top of his status to gain popularity, the supply circle will take advantage of the narcissist's need for publicity to further their own agenda, whether it's a promotion at work or special treatment. Most of the time, the narcissist is too preoccupied with knowing he is being duped before it is too late. There may be individuals in the circle who are intelligent but not as well-known as the narcissist. So they cleverly use his abilities to further their own agenda while simultaneously appeasing the narcissist. He truly claims that the narcissistic circle exists solely to applaud and encourage his accomplishments.

The narcissist, on the other hand, is quick to point out to himself that he doesn't need anybody and that the only reason people love and praise him is that they really care for him. It never occurs to him that those people may have a hidden agenda and aren't just doing it for the sake of admiration. The narcissist decides that he must focus on his supply circle and will not allow anyone in the circle to be independent. He is adamant in his conviction that the circle exists to serve him. Any signs of noncompliance with the narcissist's desires from everyone in the circle would enrage him. He is prone to anger, and it is not worth invoking his temper because if he crosses the line, he loses all sense of thought and will not calm down until he has exacted his revenge.

Rage

A narcissist is a rage-filled person. He screams for the attention he craves with this fury. He would yell at everyone in the office about trivial matters. Prepare to see a side of him that is mostly hidden when his arrogant fake self is hurt. When he suffers what he perceives to be a narcissistic injury (a threat to his carefully cultivated false self, self-esteem, and worth), his rage erupts like an angry volcano. As the anger continues to burn, the narcissist is just thinking of one thing: vengeance.

A narcissist believes he is always right and has an ego that cannot be satisfied. When anyone wrongs him or his deeds, he retaliates in the most aggressive manner possible. Rage can also be a promotional stunt for him, in which he yells his head off only to get a few people to turn around and notice that he is a big deal. It's critical to distinguish between anger and narcissistic rage.

Narcissistic rage is not triggered by traditional anger causes or circumstances that require an emotional response of anger. Ordinary rage is triggered when someone harms our loved ones or us or when we witness an open act of oppression against a marginalized person. While it is a negative trait, normal rage is selfless in its own way.

An individual should see beyond his or her own issues and advocate for others. The anger of a narcissist is his way of scaring people, and when he sees fear in their faces, he knows he has succeeded. This paranoia feeds their sadistic tendencies and solidifies their sense of value. It makes no difference to a narcissist whether or not the people around him are hurting or being treated unfairly. He might even turn a blind eye to such occurrences. And when his physical or mental self has been injured, does he become enraged. He may erupt into uncontrollable anger if even a single fingernail on his person is broken, but he is completely unconcerned if anyone is beaten to death. The narcissist has no friends or someone that you or I (normal people) would consider a close friend due to his anger. A narcissist believes that anger is his way of regaining the power of his delusional state. His public show of irrational anger is a way for him to exert power over his personal space and domain.

The Need For Control And Power

Domination is the driving force behind a narcissist's existence. He's essentially a control freak who, if he had his way, would take control of the air we breathe. He wants to manipulate anything and everyone around him because he is afraid of rejection. When he is asked for advice, he gladly gives it and then follows up on it. He will ensure that the individual follows his advice to the letter and will not encourage him to deviate from it.

When asked for an opinion or a small suggestion, he expects the individual to set aside any other thoughts he might have and obey the narcissist's instructions diligently. A narcissist's life goal is to rule over all he touches, including his office, anyone he associates with, and social gatherings. He considers control to be "power over" rather than "power with." He abuses his power and influence to perpetrate emotional and verbal violence. He loves being able to look down on people and sometimes stepping on them. From a practical standpoint, narcissists have strong control over authority, but that degree of control is not something most people might like.

The narcissist will be the only one who enjoyed the journey while in the driver's seat. He has strong ideas on how things should be done, whether at home or work. However, when it comes to putting the strategy into action, he has no desire to be involved. He thinks he is far too valuable for menial labour. So, though he has strong opinions on any minor detail, he is unconcerned about burning calories over them. He is adamant that only if he is put in the manager's chair can everything go smoothly. His definition of regulation will be to continually remind people that they aren't doing their jobs correctly. When one of his coworkers completes their job on time and in a professional manner, he only gives them half-hearted credit.

In a domestic environment, for example, he is extremely frugal, allowing him to keep a tight grip on the entire budget. He believes that any family's basic need must pass through him, and he expects people to seek his permission before doing anything. When people ask him for permission to do something, he is overjoyed. In reality, he considers it ludicrous that people will leave him out of the loop. He is swift to criticize someone that he believes is not doing things correctly, in his opinion. He reluctantly accepts credit as it is due and protests during the entire process.

In his paranoia, he assumes that, in the end, he gets all the credit because the plan's success is due to him. His philosophy entitles him to full credit for the success of any plan in which he participated, even though his contribution was negligible. On the other hand, it is the responsibility of junior officers, not him, if the strategy fails. He's just as good at taking credit for something he didn't do as he is at blaming someone for something that may or may not have been entirely his fault.

Seeks Grandiosity

This is the most noticeable and distinguishing characteristic of any narcissist. His outlook on life casts him in a heroic light while placing others on a lower plane. A narcissist deludes himself into believing that he is one of the world's most powerful people. He assumes that the events that have led up to his birth have some grand purpose or supernatural divine planning behind them. He places an unrealistically high value on his skills and abilities. A narcissist would often oversell himself by exaggerating his abilities, regardless of how talented he is. He develops a superiority complex, believing that all of his talents and skills are the greatest that anyone can have. He is consumed by himself, fantasizing about strength, achievement, and appearance, and believing that he is superior and special. He is boastful, self-centred, pretentious, and self-referential as a result of this. He spends a lot of time in his dreams, where he glorifies his life in such a grand way that he has to put up a superb front just to make his reality bearable.

To hide his lack of skill, accomplishments, skills, and power, the narcissist exaggerates his abilities, achievements, talents, and capacity in the archives of general psychiatry. Admitting that he lacks those skills that a competitor or coworker can possess damages his ego, exaggerating to dangerous levels. For such self-wounded dreams, the sky is the limit. He claims he has no limits and that he does not want anyone because of his grandiose fantasies.

Cannot Handle The Shame

There is a fine line between perfectionism and grandiosity for the narcissist. When he doesn't get what he wants, he feels insufficient. Rejection, a loss of control over his surroundings, and a lack of focus are all factors that can contribute to a feeling of futility. Interestingly, the narcissist feels inferior and full of faults as he encounters guilt. His narcissistic false self suffers accidents as a result of this. Despite all of the pomp and circumstance, a narcissist must also acknowledge the fact. This reality is often followed by feelings of guilt and an inferiority complex. The narcissist suffers a major emotional setback due to this stark contrast to his flawless dream world.

He becomes incredibly volatile and unpredictably unpredictable. At this point, he is enraged and aiming his wrath at everyone who comes close to him. He is overwhelmed by his feelings of inadequacy, exposure, and vulnerability. So, to release this negative energy, he turns on others in his immediate vicinity. The reasoning or explanation for the anger may or may not be valid. In his opinion, he seeks to divert attention away from his inferior self by engaging in mindless acts of aggression.

Desires Perfection

A narcissist is obsessed, and his false self drives his obsession. Because he is fascinated with perfection and process, he can create work of higher quality than his peers. He sets unattainable, if not outright impossible, targets for himself to accomplish. He is always struggling to achieve and attain goals due to his ambitious goals and grandiosity, and he feels a great deal of guilt when he fails. Although the tasks he set for himself may be beyond reasonable human ability, he is incapable of processing failure as something that might happen to anyone. Because of his dominance and individuality, he convinces himself that even the most messed-up strategy would succeed if he is in charge. He also feels that even though others are capable of doing it, they will never match his level of excellence.

Furthermore, when the narcissist thinks in terms of "all right or all wrong" (no middle ground) or "all white and black," all of his accomplishments must fall into one of two categories. He is not a believer in making concessions. All of his accomplishments and outcomes must be spectacular. Otherwise, he will be labelled a failure. In his eyes, accomplishments that fall short of his grandiosity are utter failures, and he has no space for improvement because he believes he knows everything there is to know in his field of research. He refuses to admit that he should change because he is already fine in every way. Every project he undertakes must result in a "eureka" moment, or it is a total failure in his eyes. He may be able to get a project to a 60%

success rate, but he will not consider it an accomplishment; instead, he may abandon the project and move on to something else in pursuit of that one path-breaking moment. When the moment occurs, he is so pleased and proud of himself that he will brag about it for years. His ego is stoked by this "eureka" moment.

When he fails to meet his objectives, his sense of perfectionism and individuality is harmed. He feels unappreciated, ashamed, and exposed. Failure enrages him, filling him with self-doubt and self-loathing. He will chastise himself, which will inflame his anger. As an ongoing tug of war between juggling grandiosity and perfectionism, he feels a great deal of guilt when he falls short of his perfectionist tendencies. Each failure adds to his already unstable state. So, if a narcissist has been failing for a long time, the odds of him losing his sanity are very high.

Constantly Bored

The narcissist is always on the lookout for new and exciting things to do in his life. He takes advantage of the enthusiasm to boost his self-esteem. An adrenaline junkie is a narcissist. They will undoubtedly leap out of a plane or attempt a bungee jump; they will seek out all sorts of thrills in the hopes of cementing their individuality and alleviating their rage. He's still on the lookout for fresh thrills. No hobby will keep him occupied for long because he will eventually tire of it.

When confronted with boredom, the narcissist will devolve into depression. He'll go to great lengths to escape depression because it evokes feelings of helplessness, despair, and a desire for love and appreciation. When he has nothing to do and no one to turn to, he can become actively involved in degrading addictive behaviours. He is still eager to try something different to avoid boredom. The fact that the practice hurts him is secondary to his primary goal of keeping himself occupied. From the perspective of a third party, it makes sense to keep a narcissist busy, preferably with something harmless to keep him off the streets. His out-of-control emotions are most likely to put himself and others in danger.

Boredom causes distress in the narcissistic individual and drains all of their energy. The narcissist can not tolerate boredom for long because of this. If the narcissist's narcissistic supply chain is unavailable, the narcissist can engage in actions that draw a ton of attention to him. He is just as eager to focus on attention as he is to be the centre of attention for himself.

Continually Seeking Fame

The narcissist is always seeking glory. He would go to any length to be in the spotlight because he believes that being in the spotlight demonstrates his peers' approval and appreciation. Much of this is done to hope that fame and eventual adoration can help fill the void left by childhood.

The insatiable desire for human interaction he missed as a child or the sense of superiority he formed as a child is the source of his relentless need for admiration. The narcissist would develop multiple personality disorder due to his ongoing battle between his real and false selves. He will break off to the personality he feels secure in when he feels ashamed, out of control, or ineffective.

It's worth noting that while the narcissist will feel guilt, it won't be directed at him; rather, it will be directed outwards, toward other people rather than the self. This is so he can avoid taking responsibility or suffering any negative consequences such as feelings of unworthiness or self-contempt. When these feelings arise, the narcissist would either retreat to his narcissistic supply or put themselves in a position that they would undoubtedly receive a lot of attention for some purpose. He feels alive, needed, and desired as a result of his celebrity.

The more he is desired, the grander he becomes, and the more narcissistic he becomes. As he is being praised, he interprets this as a confirmation of his worth, or rather, the worth of his phoney self. He becomes overconfident and verbose, going to great lengths to flaunt his newfound celebrity status. The narcissist acted under the assumption that crossing him in the wrong direction would result in revenge at this level of self-assurance and self-confidence.

CHAPTER THREE
THE DIFFERENT TYPES OF NARCISSISTIC PERSONALITY DISORDER (NPD)

Although we refer to narcissism as a general concept, there are many types. When you encounter a narcissist face to face in the real world, there might be symptoms that fit how they act because most narcissists are a combination of different forms. As in most mixes, the dominant form is often mixed with another.

Here are a quick overview of each form and their distinct characteristics or personality traits to help you figure out which one is which

Cerebral

A Cerebral narcissist assumes that they are superior to all else and that their intellect is unrivalled. They flaunt their intellect and presumption of superiority to be praised and envied by others. They are well-versed in, well, everything. They make a point of having an opinion or a suggestion on something you throw at them. They'll be able to tell you stories about how brilliant they are, whether the stories are true or made up. They are quick to point out someone else's flaws, and they will sneer and look down on everyone with a lower IQ. Such people are so concerned with their grey matter that they would go to extraordinary lengths to protect it, even to the point of jeopardizing their health and physical prowess. Sexual arousal is often linked to narcissism.

Cerebral narcissists prefer intimate stimulation over social stimulation, but they rarely participate in sexual stimulation with others. As a result, it should come as no surprise that they prefer the anonymity and lack of intimacy that pornography provides. As a result, they may prefer porn to close real-life relationships. Maintaining a relationship with people like this is a Herculean activity in and of itself. They will often insist on being the intellectually superior partner in the relationship and will assert the dominance of the other person's feelings, emotions, and behaviour. Even then, since they are still searching for more superior people to connect with, these relationships would be very short-lived. Somatic narcissists are not the same as cerebral narcissists.

Somatic

Somatic narcissists have a stronger link to the Greek legend of Narcissus. They're all overwhelmed by their own perceptions of their own beauty. Somatic narcissists are often found in gyms or other places where they are improving their appearance. It's all about their body and physique for them. They are always flexing their muscles and boasting about their athletic accomplishments. They dress immaculately and keep themselves well-groomed because they expect their body to be the source of their narcissistic supply. Their narcissistic supply comes from other people's reactions to their appearance or from their sexual conquests – most somatic narcissists would have a long list of partners.

They never stop bragging about their bedtime conquests. Even if they've had many lovers, the majority of their sex is likely to be cold and emotionless. The term "partner" eventually loses its sense, and they are better identified as "victim." You shouldn't put it past a somatic narcissist to cheat in his or her marriage. He's happiest when he can get his narcissistic fix from a variety of places. They are very dangerous because they know how to exploit people's emotions and sexual desires. If they continue to be in a long-term relationship with them, this will scar their partner for life.

Overt

Grandiosity is a form of narcissism. They are preoccupied with having exceptional success in a variety of areas, such as brilliance, attractiveness, strength, ideal love, and so on. They feel that other people can only completely understand them on their degree of grandiosity because they have such a strong sense of it. The overt narcissist must still be in command of the situation. They are never wrong, and they will never hesitate to state unequivocally that everything revolves around them and that everything must be done their way. Their egos are enormous, and they are not shy about displaying them to you.

The overt narcissist can physically or verbally harm you while showing no remorse or guilt. Such people are very exploitative of others and would not hesitate to use others to meet their own needs. They are experts at masking their egotism behind false modesty, despite the fact that they are narcissistic on the inside. They are envious of other people and are envious of their accomplishments, possessions, and relationships. They have a severe lack of empathy, which renders them unfit for group work. They are normally solitary people. They can seem overconfident, and their conduct is unmistakably extrovert; in reality, it would be better to characterize their personality as noisy, clear, larger-than-life, and authoritarian.

Covert

The covert narcissist displays all of the typical narcissistic characteristics, with one exception: they want someone to look after them. The shy type of narcissism is the best way to describe them. He has grand fantasies, much like other narcissists, but he lacks the motivation to carry them out. He lacks self-confidence and is too timid to get what he wants. He normally feels worthless because he can't do just what he wants. For the same thing, he has strong feelings of guilt. He barely acknowledges his accomplishments. He openly admires and secretly envies successful people. He cannot make acceptable friends and tends to associate with people who are of a lower calibre. Such individuals are hyper-aware of rejection and embarrassment. They could be identified as parasites that feed on the lives of others. They will almost always show symptoms of a disease that needs to be treated, which is why they will never be what you expect. They don't want to be responsible for anything, so they'll look for a powerful, successful, and intelligent partner who can run their lives without them having to contribute anything. Covert narcissists often associate with overt narcissists.

Unprincipled

The unprincipled narcissist lacks a conscience and seems to be incapable of distinguishing between right and wrong. They are unconcerned with rules, principles, or conventions, preferring to operate within the confines of the law. They manipulate others without empathy because they deem others to be inferior to them in the first place. They are more than willing to risk harm due to their irresponsible lifestyle, and they are remarkably fearless in the face of danger. Their nefarious and diabolical habits are readily apparent, and they often land them in legal trouble. They get pleasure from dominating and abusing others. These people never develop attachments to anyone and can shift from one person to the next with remarkable ease. They have no concept of emotional bonds and have no regret for losing a promising relationship. Since the narcissist is normally very charming, the people they leave crumpled in their wake are severely harmed. These narcissists are particularly dangerous because reality is only relative to them.

They are masters of deception and coercion. They are skilled at scheming behind a friendly and civil facade. Even if the means are barely justified, their plans are typically very clever and deserving of admiration. They have little regard for the wellbeing of others, no morals or scruples, and are extremely dishonest when dealing with others. They have an arrogant demeanour and are motivated by a desire to outsmart others to show that they are smarter. While many evil narcissists never come into contact with the law, this type of narcissist can be found in jails or substance recovery facilities. Keep your guard up while you're in the presence of an evil narcissist. They can scent your insecurities a mile away and use you as a scapegoat for their next heist.

Amorous

Amorous narcissists are always romantic or seductive, and they base their whole sense of self-worth on their many sexual conquests. Their relationships are always pathological, and after they have seduced another, they are likely to cast them aside to find their next conquest. They never pursue an emotional connection, preferring to inflate their already inflated ego by sexually dominating other people they regard as trophies.

The victim has little to no awareness that they are being exploited, and they might even fall in love with the narcissists. The narcissist, on the other hand, is completely devoid of empathy and would throw them away like paper towels. As a result, they're outrageous heartbreakers. They are not only known for being heartbreakers, but they will also engage in heinous acts such as pathological lying, defrauding their sexual partner of money, and other deceptions. They take advantage of their sexual prowess to deceive innocent victims. The adoring narcissist serves as a means of coping with intense feelings of inadequacy. They usually get away with it because people are hesitant to file a lawsuit against them.

Compensatory

Compensatory narcissists are often searching for a way to make up for problems in the past, such as in their youth, and they do it by creating the illusion of superiority. Rather than living in the real world, they choose to live in a fantasy world where they play the leading role in a theatre that does not exist. They make up accomplishments to boost their self-esteem. They need an audience of people who would believe their lies, and they are acutely aware of how others view them, searching for cues that they are being chastised. They strive to make up for all they believe they have been denied. Their plan is identical to that of other narcissists, except that instead of committing random acts of narcissism, they are more centred.

The Elite

In certain ways, the elite narcissist resembles the compensatory narcissist in that they are fascinated with their self-image. They continue to persuade themselves and others that they have special abilities and talents, even though the sense of self they build barely resembles the real individual. They would, more often than not, transform a partnership into a rivalry or a contest for the sole purpose of winning and proving to others that they are genuinely superior. This can happen in any relationship, whether it's family, work, or love. A social climber, the elite narcissist, would gladly step on anybody who stands in his or her way. In some ways, he is the most dangerous of all the forms because he hides so well in plain sight that even his closest associates mistake him for a decent and honest guy.

An elite narcissist is typically a highly successful businessman or woman with a well-established reputation. They place a higher priority on material wealth and properties than on true emotion. They are masters of deceit and frequently use their abilities to take advantage of others. They normally have a legitimate and reputable company that they use as a cover for all of their shady activities, being as sly as they are. They protect their personal space with their lives. They will kill you without hesitation if they even get the slightest indication that you are a threat to everything they have created. They are cruel and lack empathy and guilt. They are only concerned about their well-being and achieving their objectives. They would go to any extent to obtain their goals.

Some of the narcissistic subtypes are mentioned below. Regularly, these sub-types can be experienced by a variety of individuals. Others are irritable but tolerable, while others are harmful to one's emotional well-being.

Conversational

Have you ever been in the situation where you're talking to someone, ranting or just telling him one of your daily life stories? What's remarkable is how the dialogue always ends with him as the protagonist and victor? Isn't it annoying? It's not only nauseating to hear stories with the same happy ending, but it's also irritating that they still make you forget what you're going to tell due to their frequent interruption.

31

This type of conversation may take place amongst ordinary people, but it is almost always the case with narcissists. There are also more offensive conversational narcissists who cut you off in the middle of a sentence just so they can insist on their plot, in which the main character is always them.

Try to notice if reading this section of the book reminds you of the one person who never fails to do this every time you're in a discussion. Examine his other mannerisms, behaviours, and how he interacts with others. Most likely, you have a narcissist who is using all of his mates as supply outlets.

Group Narcissism

When the subject of narcissism comes up, we are always given the impression that it is all about a person who just cares about himself. This is right, but it does not rule out the possibility of narcissism in a group setting. The narcissist is still a member of the collective in group narcissism. The group is usually made up of narcissists who imitate themselves and have no problem coexisting. They seem to become each other's narcissistic supply source, and you'll know it's working if the party acts like a selfish individual.

Since it provides them with warmth, narcissists appear to assemble or join other narcissists in groups. This is because they are all pretty much the same and have the same attitudes or habits. There's no doubt about why he acts this way, and she acts that way because they both know they're trying to protect someone deep down inside. This community has now evolved into a guardian of each member's secret true self. Although this seems to be helpful to narcissists, it does not mean they are immune to the risk of self-destruction. It's still lurking underneath the surface.

Aggressive Or Malignant Narcissism

This is the lesser form of narcissism (classic, cerebral, somatic, elite, and others) taken to the next level to become aggressive and psychopathic. Are you familiar with Adolf Hitler or Ted Bundy? They are narcissists who are aggressive. Not all narcissists tend to damage their sources of supply or their victims physically. Much of the time, they either psychologically torment or harass you. When a narcissist gets a little too physical and commits cold-blooded murder, rape, or other crimes, that individual is already classified as a malignant or aggressive narcissist.

Destructive Narcissism

We have labels for almost every form of narcissism. To be honest, some psychologists disagree with these labels because recognizing a narcissist entails more than simply understanding the various forms and matching the various behaviours or symptoms that are dominant to that form.

Furthermore, some narcissists are so astute that they can compensate for some of their behaviours to hide them. That way, there would be less damage to the exterior, which took years and many lies to create and finish. Some people cannot be categorized as narcissists, but they can confuse you because they fit some of the narcissist's characteristics. Why am I saying all of this? This is because this form, the destructive narcissist, is one of those who do not formally suit the concept of a narcissist but exhibits general narcissist patterns.

The destructive narcissist is the only one of the four forms that seem to be a little out of the ordinary. It has some characteristics that can easily distinguish them among the different forms of narcissists, but it lacks some narcissistic traits that will solidify their narcissistic classification. Destructive narcissists normally have the most extreme narcissistic traits. Since these traits are designed to ruin and destroy those around the narcissist, they are easily associated with a pathological narcissist. However, there are fewer of the above features.

Sexual Narcissism

While this may raise your eyebrows because we know that narcissists aren't particularly fond of having sex with anyone, let us take a closer look at who these sexual narcissists are. When sex is combined with grandiosity, it becomes sexual narcissism. A sexual narcissist possesses pleasurable sexual abilities, as well as a sense of sexual superiority and a lack of sexual empathy.

What does it all mean? You get to have a romantic encounter with a sexual narcissist, but it's all for his benefit rather than yours. You can experience a sense of fulfilment, which is understandable given the narcissist's sexual abilities. However, if the narcissist believes he is already done and you aren't, he will stop, even if you are right in the middle of it. He'll just do it for you if he's in the mood. So, even if two weeks have passed, if a sexual narcissist does not feel like doing it, you will never get one.

Another factor to keep in mind about sexual narcissists is that they penchant for being unfaithful partners. What a shock! They believe that because they have all of the sexual skills, they can do it with anybody as long as they are in the mood.

Acquired Situational Narcissism (ASN)

This is a form of narcissism that is acquired over time. Since ASN is developed later in life as an adult, it is distinct from the other narcissism sub-types, including the primary ones. All other forms of narcissism are gained during a person's adolescence. ASN is not a disease that can strike someone at any time. For ASN to be successfully activated, one must have had a narcissistic propensity as a child. When a narcissistic adult comes into contact with money, celebrity status, or fame, this form of narcissism is activated. The previous pattern blossoms into a full-fledged narcissistic personality disorder, complete with signs, symptoms, attitudes, and more negative odds, much like the typical type of narcissism. The only difference is the age at which the patient was diagnosed. Their narcissistic cravings are satiated by their followers, allies, people in their immediate vicinity, false friends, assistants, social media, and conventional media.

CHAPTER FOUR
NARCISSISM IN RELATIONSHIPS

How do you recover from a narcissistic relationship?

What is the proper way to interact with another person?

If you're in some way associated with a narcissist, you'll need some protection because they all use the same tactic, and it usually doesn't end well. You may not realize it yet because of the stereotyped manner in which they work, but there is no question that you will soon enough. These Chameleons are fickle creatures that can change their minds on a dime. They are charming, and you will not realize it until it occurs, at which point they will pursue you.

When a narcissist is trying to entice others, they will appear to be loving and caring, but their facade will soon collapse. To make themselves appear better, they begin by concentrating solely on their positive qualities. This effort still fails because they are unable to conceal their contempt for the other individual. A narcissist exists in a world made of paper, where only they are worthy. In this way, they are superior to anyone else, and no matter how good the other person is, they will inevitably find faults in them and verbally harass them for not being perfect like them.

You would have taken the first step in the right direction until you have decided for yourself that you are in a relationship with a narcissist. Knowing this, you'll understand that whatever they say must be taken with a grain of salt to some extent. If you keep looking for logic in their behaviour, you'll end up going backwards, which isn't a good idea. You must defend yourself and begin to prepare for your escape using the knowledge available to you. Remember that many people believe so deeply in "marriage" that they continue to stay and take more violence, thus exacerbating the pain.

Things have changed a lot since we were children. Many people we could meet or run into in the local store or gas station could be counted on to like us back then—people who are kind, safe, and loving. In a nutshell, they were ordinary. Regrettably, the status quo has shifted. Things are no longer dependable nowadays. The impact of video games, Hollywood films, critically acclaimed social media, and the disappearance of the two-parent family has created a massive chasm that is a terrifying place to fall into. It's there, and if you go outside, you could come face to face with it.

So don't be shocked if this occurs; be prepared! Take action to gain a better understanding of how these people think and function. It's unlike anything you've ever seen or seen before, and there are resources you can use when confronted with this strange new society.

The line is that narcissistic relationships are on the rise. They should be avoided like the plague. Narcissists are sick people, but neither you nor I are. Knowing this is the first step in coping with a narcissistic relationship crisis or assisting a friend who is dealing with one.

Narcissistic people often have narcissistic parents who wished for their child to grow up to be truly exceptional, greater than anyone else. The stereotype trend for a narcissistic living can be seen here. Be better than anyone else, look down on everyone who isn't as good as you, and look for flaws in everything and everyone. But never, ever, ever, ever, ever, ever, ever, ever, ever, ever, ever, ever, ever, ever, For them, this is against the law.

The parent narcissist, like the adult narcissist, is often too preoccupied with themselves to devote enough time to the child for the simple parenting required to raise a safe and well-balanced adult. This, in turn, produces a carbon copy adult whose actions, if given a chance, would generate yet another narcissist in their child, and so on.

You can take steps if you are a reasonably stable minded person in a relationship with a narcissist to define your program for your mental wellbeing and sanity. Don't try to "fix" your narcissist; that's a job for a therapist, and you've got your own life to live. Telling them that they must do it a certain way, your way, would almost certainly aggravate your narcissist, leading to even more bad conduct. Remember that the dilemma is that you already have your hands full dealing with their bad conduct, so don't make it harder for yourself.

If you have the energy and believe in your heart of hearts that you love this guy, there are ways to make your relationship work, but it will be work. Make no mistake: getting out of a toxic relationship is much easier than staying in one.

If you decide to stick with it, the rules are very strict in terms of day-to-day life. In this game, there are no "near enough" rules. You will begin to believe that you are the one who is playing games, but keep in mind that your narcissist will manipulate you at any turn, so being sweet and pretending that all will be fine will never work for you.

Here are a few activities you can engage in to help you and your narcissist live a more "calm" life. In the end, you will be manipulating them rather than the other way around, as narcissists have always done and will continue to do.

- Never reveal the plan to them. They'll use it against you right away.
- Be familiar enough with your narcissist partner to know what works and what doesn't.
- If necessary, spend some time figuring out what works before implementing your strategy.
- Be well-prepared. Narcissists have a wide range of tricks up their sleeves to pull on you.
- Recognize the signs of "incoming" fire.
- Don't get caught up in their game-playing chat.
- If you're not sure what's going on, look away and act uninterested. BE DISINTERESTED!
- Just express your love to them while they are calm and peaceful. They are the least arrogant at those moments.

How to Heal After A Narcissistic Relationship

When you realize you're in a toxic relationship and take action to get out of it, you're the smart one, not the poor ones. We all have powerful survival instincts, and the "little voices" that tell us "this is wrong" or "get out and get out now" are there for a reason. Relationships with narcissists and other forms of toxic people are harmful to your health. There are no other words for it. Don't think about how it happened or who is to blame; just stop it, and stop it now for your own sanity's sake.

This is a movie that we've all seen before. You believe you are in love, and you want to be in love; you don't want your heart to be broken. You can use powerful words on yourself to make you understand what the best thing to do is and why you need to do it.

If you're in a poor relationship and you're aware of it, you're in pain. If you're in pain, consider the following:

Question: What can you get when you're in pain?

Answer: More suffering!

Solution: Choose happiness!

Life is a set of decisions to be made. You have the ability to choose. It is entirely up to you to make your decision.

Do you see what I'm getting at? The response is clear when you "get out" of your situation and pretend to be a doctor, "looking back in" on your toxic situation.

You'd never want to be in agony! The whole concept is absurd. But you're still there? To summarize, being in a toxic relationship does not always imply that you are a bad person. Leaving a toxic relationship will make you a happier person!

How To Spot Emotional Predators And Knowing The Red Flags Before It Is Too Late

Dating an emotional predator like a narcissist, sociopath, or psychopath can damage the emotional roller coaster. While many perpetrators take a long time to disclose their true self after they've trapped their victims, there are some tell-tale signs to watch for while dating someone who can predict their future conduct. It's important to remember that emotional abusers aren't people who act out of their suffering on occasion; they're toxic people who go out of their way to find victims and targets to achieve their goals. They have a long history of deception and coercion, as well as a lack of empathy and regret for their behaviour. Many people don't realize that this kind of conduct is planned, sadistic, and sometimes premeditated.

The nice thing about dating is that you're not committing to a relationship, so you can use it to learn more about a potential partner and, if appropriate, break ties if he or she turns out to have manipulative characteristics without putting any more time and effort into the relationship. Here are several warning signs to keep an eye out for.

1. A desire to be in control.

Abusers want to dominate and exploit their victims, so they'll find sneaky ways to keep psychological control over you. They can retain power in a variety of ways, including:

Excessive contact is a problem. Excessive flattery and attention from a charming manipulator is a means of control since it keeps you dependent on their praise, something many people are unaware of. Keep an eye out for other signals if you're being bombarded with text messages, calls, voicemails, chats, and e-mails on an hourly basis in the early stages of dating. It might seem unbelievable that someone is so enamoured with you after just one date, but it's a warning sign of questionable conduct and unwarranted attachment. It's unusual to be in touch with someone 24 hours a day, seven days a week, particularly if you've only been on a few dates with them. No one has time to regularly "check-in" with someone they're "only" dating. This type of interaction is ideal for abusers to "check-in" with you to see what you're up to, to ensure that you're sufficiently "hooked" to their attention, and it's a sort of "idealization" that puts you on a pedestal that seems irresistible at first. Of course, if you're familiar with narcissists' brutal abuse cycle, which involves idealization, devaluation, and discard, you'll be aware that you'll be knocked off your pedestal fast.

*A **negative reaction to rejection or setbacks**.* Unlike dating partners who are genuinely happy to see you again and show their interest politely, toxic partners will become enraged if you choose not to react to them right away or if you avoid their idealization by giving yourself the room you need. They won't wait for your answer, either: they'll keep following you and paying you undue attention even though they don't know much about you. This level of attentiveness isn't "flattering" at all, despite how it might seem at first—downright, it's creepy and risky. It shows a sense of entitlement to your time and presence, regardless of your interests, wishes, or desires. When you set limits with a potentially abusive partner, you can count on them being broken. And if you tell them you don't want to go home with them on a first date, they may continue to bother you despite your refusal. Be wary if your "no" always seems to be a negotiation with someone you're dating. This indicates that you are in the company of someone who does not respect your right to make your own decisions and protect your boundaries and values.

Physical Aggression. Abusers will overstep their victims' physical space because they are constant boundary-breakers. Although this form of conduct does not surface until months into a relationship, offenders may be physically abusive with you as early as the first few dates. Grabbing you too firmly, pushing you during a dispute or confrontation, infringing on your boundaries in some way, manipulating you for sex, or touching you inappropriately without your permission are all red flags that should be taken seriously. It's a warning that things are just going to get worse. You're not sure what to make of this physical assault, which could occur when you're under the influence of alcohol or other substances, so you don't know what to make of it except that you feel threatened and dangerous. Don't try to explain it by claiming that it occurs with or without alcohol—alcohol can lower inhibitions, but it doesn't cause personality changes. Even if the abuser claims that the "drink" made him or she do it, the abuser may be exposing his or her true nature.

Mistreating Others. Some people's mistreatment Even if the abuser successfully idealizes you in the early stages of dating, you will notice his or her actions toward others as a warning sign of future behaviour. Is he or she rude to the waiter or waitress on your date, for example? Is he or she easily enraged if someone else flirts with you, speaks to you, or hits on you in front of them? What about the way they discuss others? Recognize that if they deem their ex a "crazy psychopath" and use a litany of expletives about their obnoxious coworker, they have toxic temper problems that you may inevitably face. Abusers use unwarranted rage as a powerful tool to

- ➤ maintain their self-image and ego,
- ➤ project blame onto others,
- ➤ reclaim control by recreating a "version of events" that makes them seem superior and saintly, and
- ➤ elicit fear and bully others into doing what they want.

2. Addicted To Provoking You.

Provocation is a skill that covert manipulators excel at. They are investigating the weak points as they learn more about you and tailoring their remarks to what they feel would affect you the most. Knowing that their remarks have activated you gives them a sadistic sense of pleasure, as it alleviates their hidden inferiority and strokes their illusions of grandeur, power, and aptitude. They will easily manipulate you and persuade you that you don't deserve any better if they leverage your emotions.

Demeaning comments. Comments that are demeaning to your personality, appearance, line of work, what you should wear, and who you should hang out with are all unacceptable, particularly when you are just getting to know someone. Be vigilant if you find yourself being bombarded with these ostensibly "helpful" remarks constantly during the first few dates. Nobody should try to "transform" you right away because they're just getting to know you. After all, if they do, it'll be a disaster. These provocative remarks can be disguised as constructive feedback or "only jokes," but you can spot them because they often contain condescension rather than sensitivity and consideration. Harsh teasing, which is used to flirt and establish rapport with a partner, is different from playful teasing, which is used to spark your anger or frustration, bring you down, and taunt you.

Sarcasm. Be wary of the covert cynical put-downs. One of the most powerful weapons in an abuser's arsenal is sarcasm. Emotional predators take pleasure in discrediting your views, beliefs, and feelings by making cruel comments that shame you into never challenging them again. Abusers use sarcasm to avoid responsibility for their cruel, condescending tone and belittling actions because sarcasm isn't always deemed "abusive" by society. Throughout the relationship, they become increasingly condescending in their approach to sarcasm. What was once a "playful" ironic joke has become frequent emotional terrorism that questions your right to have an opinion that differs from theirs.

Attempts to make you envious. Run if your date brings up previous romantic partners often on your dates (while furtively checking to see if you're watching them while doing so), and talks about having a romantic "sort" that is very different from your definition. A good partner would try to make you feel safe and valued, rather than vulnerable and uncertain. This may be a type of toxic triangulation in which an abusive partner tries to project a desirable image while demeaning your accomplishments to motivate you to fight for his or her attention.

The silent treatment. If you challenge their authority or bring up their mistreatment, abusers will withdraw into silence. This will lead you to pursue them even harder in an attempt to persuade them to "validate" your feelings and accept that they are wrong. Unfortunately, by doing so, you are just giving them more strength. They'll finally warm up to you, but only after you've vented and apologised for being too "harsh," even though you've done nothing wrong but express yourself.

3. Character and actions that are inconsistent.

Most professional abusers will save their "hot and cold" tactics for long-term relationships. Still, other abusers will show you a sample of this behaviour as early as the first month of dating. They do this by using the following methods:

Gaslighting and projection. Gaslighting and projection are methods used by narcissistic dating partners and other abusive individuals to persuade society that their victims are insane and persuade their victims that their experience is false. Since the long-term effects of this form of coercion on victims are extremely deadly, it's critical to recognize warning signs early in the dating process so that you can separate more easily from the new type of reality that these toxic partners are likely to inflict on you.

Gaslighting and projection are two very clever techniques that allow toxic dating partners to pass the blame for their own traits onto you while still avoiding responsibility for their hypocrisy, deception, and other unsavoury conduct. Know that narcissists love calling others "crazy," so if you're uncomfortable with something your dating partner did or said and then refuted, minimized, or projected onto you, remember that narcissists enjoy calling others "crazy." It's a term they'll also use to characterize any legitimate emotional response victims have to their shady and contradictory conduct.

In its most basic form, gaslighting is a type of psychological torture in which the victim begins to doubt his or her own knowledge of the covert abuse and becomes unable to trust his or her own facts. To retain leverage, stonewalling (shutting down dialogue before it starts), silent treatments and devaluation are used. When their conduct is pointed out, narcissists can easily preserve the image of their false selves and discredit their victims, ensuring that the subtle violence is never noticed or discussed without the dire implications of you walking on eggshells.

Look at their acts rather than their words to tell the difference between a partner who gives you constructive criticism or actually disagrees with you and a partner who regularly projects their own attributes and gaslights you. Is it common for the person you're dating to accuse you of the same attributes, qualities, or behaviours that they seem to be guilty of? Do they deem you a hypocrite because they often contradict their own beliefs? Do they react by bringing up something unrelated you did to turn the focus back to you when you call them out on being rude?

You may meet narcissistic partners who are initially very possessive of you, watch where you go and who you are with, appear to check up on you 24/7, and call you out if you show signs of flirtation or engaging with another guy. However, if you ever point out signs of possible infidelity on their part or question any lies that don't add up, they might erupt in narcissistic rage and gaslight you into thinking you're the jealous, possessive one, telling you that you're getting too invested in the relationship too soon—neglecting the fact that they've been spying on you from the beginning.

Be careful—narcissists' projection and gaslighting are so sweet, so sneaky, so conniving, and so persuasive that you'll sometimes find yourself apologizing for still being alive.

Charming on the surface. There is an infinite number of toxic people who start their schemes with superficial charm, self-absorption, and a genuine lack of empathy or substance. Once you've had some experience recognizing nonverbal gestures, patterns in facial expressions, and tone of voice, you'll be able to tell how shallow their demeanours are. Skilled predators can be very charming, and you can quickly spot them by watching how they exaggerate their feelings for you and their glib ways of showing you that they "care" when they don't. On a first or second date, for example, hearing "I've never thought this way about someone else" is not only premature, but it's also most definitely a lie intended to impress you. When this charisma is combined with behaviour that contradicts the abuser's words, such as the fact that despite being so "enamoured" with you, this person never really asks you about your interests or passions, you'll quickly realize these are all superficial ways of getting into your head.

Pathological Lying. Do you ever catch the person telling lies or telling stories that don't add up? Do they "drip-feed" your details so that you can piece together the whole story over time? He used to call a girl he hung out with a "female pal," but now he says he used to date her. A man she meets for Sunday brunch is initially thought to be a colleague, but it turns out to be an ex-husband. True, everyone saves some important details from the first few dates for later, and everyone makes mistakes or tells "white lies" to protect their self-image. However, if these lies seem to be a recurring trend, it's not a good way to start a relationship. The abuser, who lives in a world of lies, has never heard of disclosure, transparency, or open communication.

Frequent Disappearances. Initially, the person you were dating was constantly on top of you, constantly calling and texting you. They suddenly vanish for days, only to reappearance as if nothing had happened. These disappearances, which are frequently staged without convincing explanations, are a method of controlling your expectations and making you "pink" for contact.

> Attitudes toward you change. Abusers think in black-and-white terms, which leads to emotional polarization in their perceptions of you. If you satisfy their needs, you're "the one," but if you disappoint them or challenge their fragile sense of dominance, you're instantly the villain. This "hot and cold" conduct should be avoided because it's just another way to control your standards and keep you on your toes. If you're the people-pleasing type, you might fall into the trap of attempting to escape rejection and win

their favour, even if you don't like them. It's the epitome of "reverse psychology."

Reinforcement that comes in waves. This is a psychological trick that makes you want to satisfy a toxic person, even though they are mistreating you. The abuser gets to keep you on your "best behaviour" without having to change his or her own. Abusers enjoy offering "crumbs" after seducing their victims with the promise of a whole loaf of bread. You could be showered with praise, flattery, and attention one day, only to be met with cold silence the next. To manage their "triggers," or their false sense of superiority when challenged, narcissists believe you should walk on eggshells. You might get the same idealization you got on the first few dates, but more often than not, you'll get a combination of hot and cold, leaving you unsure about the relationship's future

DATING SUGGESTIONS FOR DEALING WITH PREDATORS:

Do not continue if you find any of these red flags after a few dates or during the first few months of dating. Since you normally meet with a person's best actions during the first few dates, you can be sure that things will not get any better. You can't fix this guy, and you risk emotionally investing in someone trying to hurt you on purpose.

- **Be cautious.** If you flatly refuse an abuser, he or she can become enraged and use "pity ploys" or angry harassment to get you to go out with them again. If someone is annoying you, bullying you, or making you feel insecure in some way, going No Contact is a safer strategy. Block their phone number and any other contact information they might have. They don't get a friendly answer if they've been rude. If they try to threaten you, log the facts and inform them that legal action will be taken if necessary. If you're trying online dating, make sure you ban the predator from the web after you've taken screenshots of their posts.

- **When dating someone young, tread carefully.** Don't give out personal details such as your address, home phone number, or other contact information other than your cell phone number. While still getting to know others, use an option such as a Google Voice number or another text messaging program. You must prioritize your own protection and privacy.

- **Avoid gaslighting and projection.** Don't stray from what you already believe to be real. Allowing your toxic dating partner to downplay or dismiss stuff he or she might have said or done is not a good idea. When a dating partner tries to gaslight you or project attributes onto you, be aware that this is a direct sign of emotional immaturity and is not appropriate for a long-term relationship. Keeping a journal during your dating phase will help you keep track of any discrepancies, red flags, thoughts, and/or gut feelings that occur. To stay grounded in your own experiences and inner sense of reality, you'll want to return to this journal frequently.

- **Keep an open mind.** Be able to acknowledge both the positive and the poor. Although we all want to see the best of people, we must not be fooled into ignoring or downplaying the signs that anyone is incompatible with us. The signs will always be there, and even if they aren't as obvious, your gut instinct will always warn you that something isn't quite right.

Is He Or She A Narcissist, A Traumatized Person, Or Simply Emotionally Unavailable? The Differences Between "Normal" And Abusive Relationships

Outsiders who have never encountered this type of abuse may find narcissistic abuse a difficult concept to understand. Readers may be unsure whether they're dealing with a malignant narcissist or a typical young, emotionally inaccessible jerk. Let's be clear: narcissistic violence is not a complaint about incompatibility or mere emotional unavailability in relationships, nor is it a complaint about oversensitivity to the usual ups and downs of relationships. To some degree, all narcissists, sociopaths, and psychopaths are emotionally unavailable, but not all emotionally unavailable individuals are narcissists, sociopaths, or psychopaths. Their desire to hurt, their unwillingness to improve, and their sadistic nature distinguish them.

A Word on Narcissism and Complex PTSD

Given what we know about trauma and its impact on the brain, as well as studies showing how domestic violence affects the growth of abusers and abuse victims in future generations, it's reasonable to conclude that toxic people are often traumatized, injured, and in pain. From the moment we meet schoolyard bullies to the time we learn our spouse, parent, family member, coworker, or friend could be a toxic bully, we hear the phrase "Hurt people, hurt people." We make all kinds of excuses about how someone is just acting out of their own pain, how they are actually lashing out, and how they couldn't really harm others if they hadn't been hurt themselves.

However, given everything we already know about how a malignant narcissist purposefully sabotages and caters to their victim's deepest insecurities and wounds, the platitude "hurt people, hurt people" is clearly insufficient. In the chapter "The Common Myths Surrounding Narcissism," we said that not all narcissistic abusers come from a history of violence and that many grandiose narcissists do believe they have the right to harm others; some might be overvalued rather than devalued by their parents. The reality is that these types of offenders will continue to assault and will not seek psychological help because they believe that harming others rewards them.

Although early childhood trauma may have affected a person's character, it does not excuse the continuation of negative behaviour toward others in adulthood. Nonetheless, distinguishing between a traumatized and a toxic individual is a difficult task fraught with nuances, unanswered questions, and contradictory proof. Having interacted with a large number of Complex PTSD survivors and having experienced Complex PTSD myself, I've come across this issue several times and have yet to find a definitive response. Some Borderlines, for example, are misdiagnosed when they should have been diagnosed with Complex PTSD, according to Pete Walker. What distinguishes those with Complex PTSD from those with Narcissistic Personality Disorder or Antisocial Personality Disorder is how they behave out of their past trauma. How do we say if it's one or the other? What if there's anyone on the loose with all three?

We can never be certain what our loved ones are suffering from without a clinician's diagnosis. Still, we can make informed guesses based on their past and present actions, history of violence, their willingness to enter care, and so on. I believe certain defining characteristics can help us understand how someone suffering from Complex PTSD differs from someone suffering from malignant narcissism:

1. Their desire to not only accept responsibility for their decisions but also to learn from them. Malignant narcissists seldom accept full responsibility for their decisions, preferring to escape accountability wherever possible. If they don't have co-morbid malignant narcissistic tendencies, complex PTSD patients are frequently lost in a sea of self-blame and toxic guilt, blaming themselves for all the trauma they've experienced. While Complex PTSD survivors may be triggered and lash out, they do not use their illness as an excuse to avoid taking responsibility for their acts. Instead, they seek assistance and enrol in rehab, as well as admit when they have harmed others.

2. Their capacity to empathize with others and express sincere regret for their harmful actions. Malignant narcissists are known for having a limited spectrum of emotions and a reduced capacity for empathy. Many of the trauma survivors I know who aren't malignant narcissists are extremely empathic, and as a result of what has happened to them, they want to prevent it from happening to others. Unlike malignant and violent narcissists who are in a constant state of "war" and wish to preemptively assault others, a trauma survivor's hurtful conduct is not deliberate or catered to the wounds of others but rather stems from a sense of threat and the need to self-isolate. Harming people, sometimes inadvertently, causes them a lot of pain and sends them into a downward spiral of negative self-talk.

3. The person has been exposed to visible traumas that have occurred recently or have surfaced due to a smaller trauma that has triggered a series of larger traumas from childhood. Although narcissistic offenders can have a

history of trauma, a survivor with Complex PTSD has always had the worst of both worlds: being abused as an infant, only to be abused again as an adult. It's not because they're malignant narcissists that they're acting uncharacteristically against their perpetrators or because they're emotionally overwhelmed; it's because they're still recovering from the trauma's effect.

4. Trauma survivors who do not have a history of manipulating others do not abuse or belittle others on purpose; rather, their actions stem from a desire to defend themselves rather than degrade others. Be cautious: some malignant narcissists may appear to have PTSD or Complex PTSD when harassing and manipulating others, but they are dealing with something much deeper and darker than trauma symptoms. Complex PTSD survivors who aren't narcissistic would not go out of their way to intimidate, degrade, or hurt others (in fact, they're hyperaware of their effect because they've been abused); however malignant narcissists will.

5. They seek psychological help and work to change their conduct to reduce the damage and effect their actions have on others. Malignant narcissists are so rewarded for their actions that they either avoid treatment or deceive therapists into believing they are the victims rather than the people they have harmed. Non-narcissistic Complex Trauma survivors come to therapy with a sincere desire to overcome their destructive attitudes, both to themselves and others. Many who have experienced complex trauma are more likely to engage in self-harm and self-defeating actions, while malignant narcissists are more likely to harm others.

The overlaps, disparities, and complexities between Complex PTSD and malignant narcissism are complex. Still, I hope you can see the distinctions clearly—intent to hurt others versus self-harm, empathy, a broad emotional spectrum, evolution, and the desire to improve and take responsibility for one's behaviour are all distinguishing factors. When people are traumatized, they can exhibit narcissistic tendencies and behaviors that are not representative of who they are. Malignant narcissists, on the other hand, have had a consistent pattern of behaviour since childhood, regardless of whether or not they have experienced trauma.

Another question I often get is whether survivors of narcissistic violence will go on to become narcissists. It depended on whether you mean when you were a kid or when you were an adult. According to my understanding, narcissism is a childhood personality disorder. So if a scapegoat or golden kid did become narcissistic as a result of the central wound or upbringing that disrupted their habits of behaving and communicating, it's entirely plausible that a child might become narcissistic, if not a full-fledged narcissist.

However, an adult that has been traumatized by a narcissistic spouse is unlikely to develop NPD in the future because NPD is a condition that develops during adolescence, most likely as a result of a combination of a biological predisposition and environmental factors. The abuse survivor is more likely to pick up "fleas," or transient narcissistic habits, and/or suffer from the trauma. As a defensive mechanism against violence, flea-like habits are picked up. Children of narcissistic parents who do not grow up to be full-fledged narcissists will pick up on fleas from their encounters without being full-fledged narcissists. Again, a malignant narcissist is defined by a lack of capacity for empathizing, developing, taking responsibility, and planning and desiring to hurt others, not by the occasional toxic action or characteristic.

Apart from the distinctions between traumatized and toxic people, a line must be drawn between a natural, healthy relationship (or even just a "regular" unhealthy one in which both parties contribute to toxicity) and a toxic, abusive relationship in which the abuser wields a significant amount of control. The violence mentioned in this book is not ordinary jealousy, rage, or healthy conflict that leads to resolution and development in a relationship; it results from an individual with a personality disorder repeatedly devaluing, controlling, sabotaging, and disrespecting a victim. It's also not something that can be "worked out" since malignant narcissists refuse to adjust because their coercive conduct benefits them.

If you've witnessed a narcissistic abuser's intentional cruelty (as in, they fed off your pain and made sure to provoke you where it hurt) using the methods I've mentioned in this book, coupled with a complete lack of empathy, your partner may be on the narcissistic continuum, even if they aren't a full-fledged narcissist. If, on the other hand, you believe this partner might empathize but did not want to be in a close relationship, it could be due to emotional unavailability or compatibility problems. These individuals can be extremely frightening and dangerous; many survivors would prefer to meet a normal emotionally unavailable person over a full-fledged narcissist every day. While the former is unquestionably painful, the latter is always harmful.

It's impossible to tell if this partner has a full-fledged personality disorder without knowing the partner's entire range of conduct, which is mostly witnessed throughout a very close, long-term relationship, but it may appear earlier. Many outsiders never get close enough to a narcissistic partner to discover the mask by devaluation and discard, so they never know who is behind the mask.

What you might have seen is just a sliver of this person's personality, implying that there is far more underneath the surface. How narcissists behave in long-term romantic relationships differ from those in short-term relationships since the long-term partner is often subjected to a horrible cycle of violence. In contrast, the short-term partner can often be subjected to horrific abuse, but the cycle is thankfully cut short before the victim can live through the entire, prolonged nightmare.

Let me say it again: narcissistic abuse, or any sort of abuse, is not a "relationship" problem. It's not just a matter of incompatibility, or the occasional toxic communication problem, or the usual human defects that all of us have. It's not a problem that can be solved by modifying and improving ourselves, even though self-change is necessary because none of us is perfect and could all use some improvement.

The problem isn't with imperfection because we're all imperfect in some way. Relationships are complicated enough without violence, but when abuse is present, the relationship is no longer a relationship. It's a con—a sly con man or con woman seducing us into believing we're in a relationship to manipulate our emotions.

The problem is that the victim's imperfection, or perceived imperfection, is an excuse for unjustified violence. Victims are often persuaded by their spouses that their very human weaknesses (or flaws invented by the narcissist to create insecurity) are somehow deal-breaker personality traits. Consider how a non-abusive partner will never have to abuse you to give you constructive criticism, work through a disagreement, or break down a barrier. A non-abusive partner would handle incompatibility in a better way, either by negotiating with you to fix the problems or by ending the relationship maturely if they thought you and your partner were not a good match.

Yeah, unhealthy relationships result from the personality characteristics and toxic experiences between two individuals, but being in a relationship with a narcissistic abuser goes beyond that. It crosses the line into intentional psychological (and often physical) fear and violence—outrageous acts of cruelty and inhumanity. It's unfathomable to those who haven't been through it, but all too true for those who have.

The problem isn't a victim's oversensitivity to the abuser's violence or indifference; regardless of how sensitive a victim is, an abuser's intentionally hurtful and deceptive actions will harm them their level of confidence. Do you expect a child who is constantly broken down and belittled by a narcissistically abusive parent to have the same degree of trust after these childhood experiences? No, it's not true. What about an adult who has had traumatic encounters in a decade-long marriage with a narcissist or who has already been exploited as a child and re-experiences it? Do you believe they'll be the same person? No, it's not true. For both children and adults, narcissistic violence is traumatic and life-changing—especially for children who have been emotionally abused and bruised, only to be used as a punching bag again by their adult spouses. If you find a way to use your trust and protection to end the relationship and begin to recover from it, no amount of confidence or security can completely shield you from the pain of chronic trauma.

Narcissist or Emotionally Unavailable?

I'm often asked whether there are any distinctions between emotionally unavailable people and narcissists. While all full-fledged narcissists are emotionally unavailable by nature, not all emotionally unavailable people are full-fledged narcissists, as I previously mentioned. Their narcissism can be transient or coincidental, but it can still be toxic to those around them. Without meeting the full requirements for this condition, emotionally unavailable individuals or smooth-talking players will blow hot and cold, be superficially charming, vanish without a word, use sporadic encouragement (both deliberately and inadvertently due to the many other people they're chasing at the same time), and have a harem.

They can still feel empathy towards others while being manipulative and unwilling to join abusive relationships, unlike narcissists. Even if they have the potential to feel guilty for their decisions and the ability to change if they want to, they will always come off as toxic. Being emotionally unavailable may be a defensive mechanism for the hurt they've suffered in the past, not to explain their behaviour. If they don't take the time and space to process and repair their trauma, even survivors of narcissistic violence may become emotionally inaccessible. That doesn't mean they're malignant narcissists; it just means they've been traumatized and don't have the best relationship contact habits. Emotional unavailability and recovery from the effects of trauma aren't always life sentences, but a narcissistic abuser's lack of empathy that refuses to alter is.

On the other side, we must keep in mind that these perpetrators may be narcissists who act remorseless. It can be difficult to tell them apart at this stage. Normally, what will set them apart is how they behave before and after a breakup—do they launch a smear campaign? Do they look for a new partner right away? Do they try to reach you even though you have a new partner? Do they seem to be able to dismiss you without saying anything? Is it apparent that they stage personal attacks on you in the relationship, stonewalling, chronic emotional invalidation, and gaslighting? Is it common for them to triangulate you with others? Do they follow you around if you leave because of a narcissistic injury? Should they strictly adhere to the idealization, devaluation, and discard phases? There are signals that something more serious is going on than emotional unavailability.

While narcissists are more likely to use such strategies than others, such as triangulation, emotional bullies of any type (with or without other disorders such as Antisocial Personality Disorder) may still be manipulative and toxic. They may have a variety of other issues, such as rage issues, addictions, control issues, and envy issues, that are unrelated to the condition. That is why, even if they aren't full-fledged narcissists, they aren't worth pursuing in the long run and can harm your mental health.

I understand how difficult it is to be emotionally unavailable. It's toxic and dysfunctional, and dating an emotionally unavailable person who doesn't know what he or she wants is never enjoyable. It can be sad and frightening at the same time. But, and this is a big but, even your average emotionally inaccessible jerk who isn't a malignant narcissist or sociopath will evolve. They aren't typically manipulative in the same way that a malignant narcissist is. You may also move on and evolve from an emotionally unavailable person with some closure, accepting they were not the right person for you. He or she may be selfish, traumatized, or just not interested in commitment—who knows what their problem is? When malignant narcissism is added to the mix, however, a whole new set of problems emerges.

Narcissistic abuse is a pattern of contempt, devaluation, and deterioration that occurs over time. It's all about psychological warfare and deception. It always entails losing sight of your goals, finances, and, in some cases, even your sanity and life. I'm not exaggerating when I say that this type of violence has a life-long impact—I've learned from thousands of survivors all over the world who have been mentally, physically, financially, and spiritually drained by these toxic individuals. They've been beaten in every way possible, and as you'll see in the first few pages of this novel, some of them have been driven over the edge— victims of a silent crime in which the perpetrators are barely kept responsible for their deeds, or are only held accountable until it's far too late.

Survivors of this type of clandestine violence sometimes feel as though they have no one to turn to. Psychological abuse is increasingly being exposed by mental health practitioners and advocates, but not at a point where every therapist is aware of the complexities. I would warn any marriage or couple's therapists to be careful of these people, as they are very good at convincing therapists that the victim is the abuser. Friends and family members may be the abusers themselves, or they may easily dismiss the perspectives of survivors because they may fail to recognize exactly what is going on until they have witnessed it themselves. I've heard far too many stories about the criminal justice system, victims' friends and family members, and the malignant narcissist's harem members siding with the abuser over the victim—all because of their false mask.

Remember how, before learning about narcissistic violence, you were prone to excusing, denying, justifying, or rationalizing your abuser's behaviour. You may have blamed yourself for "provoking" the abuser in some way as a victim of violence because that is what the abuser wanted you to believe. It's difficult to understand why this isn't a regular or even a typical dysfunctional relationship since the latter normally involves two dysfunctional people who don't know how to interact in a healthy way. In reality, you were unlikely to have told anybody the whole truth about what you were going through while in an abusive relationship because you were afraid they wouldn't believe you.

Unfortunately, they do not believe you, and this has to do with how we stigmatize violence survivors in society, making them feel ashamed of the fact that they were abused, to begin with. As a coping strategy, many victims try to "play up" intimate moments with their perpetrators to others or highlight everything that is going well, in order to appear as if everything is perfect while, behind closed doors, the survivor is battling for survival every day of his or her life. This is also why it's so easy for a narcissist to swoop in and work his or her magic, telling everyone who will listen that the victim is "unhinged" and that the narcissistic abuser did "so much" for them while the victim remained silent for years.

The instability in an abusive relationship is largely due to the abuser's behavioural habits, but the consequences of trauma can definitely cause the survivor to engage in maladaptive coping strategies and lash out in ways that are out of character for them. The victim can attempt to cope with the trauma in a variety of ways, including attempting to reclaim their control by employing tactics similar to those employed by a narcissist, but without engaging in them as heartlessly. As a result, they become increasingly embarrassed, and the abuser then uses their actions to justify the violence, despite the fact that the abuser knows full well that the victim would not have responded in this manner if they had never been abused in the first place for such a long time.

Just because a survivor becomes reactive after a period of prolonged disrespect does not render the dynamic "mutual violence." It's important to note that the victim has been traumatized and is then gradually activated by the narcissist. To survive, they can resort to some maladaptive coping mechanisms. The victim of this form of violence must then take responsibility for finding healthier coping mechanisms, but this does not make the victim the abuser (even though the abuser will certainly try to convince them they are). The victim enters the relationship intending to love and care for someone in a mutual relationship; the offender enters the relationship as a con artist, someone who gradually but steadily erodes the victim's reality, manipulating the victim for all they are worth. The victim attempts to over-communicate and articulate his or her emotions to their abuser to no avail, trying to express how much the abuser has affected them. In contrast, the abuser "hovers" the victim back in with pity ploys, false expressions of guilt, or hollow apologies that never include changes in actions or empathy for the victim.

The bottom line is that emotionally unavailable people come in all shapes and sizes. Survivors of complex PTSD and trauma, as well as victims of narcissists, will evolve. They have a strong capacity for empathy and guilt. They not only know right from wrong, but they can also tell the difference when it comes to their actions. Narcissists with a malignancy? They don't give a damn about the people they hurt in the process. Every one of us has undoubtedly engaged in a toxic act or two at some point in our lives, but that doesn't mean we're abusive or toxic narcissists on a long-term basis. We are just human, but we do not deserve to be mistreated.

If you want to know if you're in trouble, ask yourself if you're being exploited mentally, physically, financially, sexually, or in some other way. If you answered yes, the issue is more complicated than incompatibility or emotional unavailability. Whether or not an individual is a true malignant narcissist becomes less important than their long-term pattern of behaviour—even when labels fail—their long-term behaviour will tell you everything you need to know.

CHAPTER FIVE
EFFECTS OF NARCISSISM ON FAMILY AND CHILDREN

It's what Sigmund Freud called repetition compulsion, and it's what I call childhood subconscious programming. It's where we get all of our icky patterns (I'm sure that's the psychiatric term) of adulthood entanglement with narcissistic partners and friends after growing up with narcissistic parents. Not every narcissistic abuse victim has been abused as a child; in fact, I've met many survivors who were never abused as children. This demonstrates that anyone can be a target of a narcissist because many are subtle and insidious, and you might not realize you're in a relationship with one until it's too late.

We can't deny, though, that being "pre-programmed" for the violence of some sort from a young age can have a detrimental effect on our interpersonal relationships. We should recognize these tendencies without blaming ourselves in the process.

Childhood trauma, such as emotional deprivation or rape, may have alarmingly powerful effects on our psychology as we grow older, even to the point of rewiring the brain. Children of narcissistic parents, those who meet the medical criteria for Narcissistic Personality Disorder, know all too well what it's like to be raised by someone who lacks empathy and has an unhealthy sense of grandiosity, false superiority, and entitlement. Children of narcissistic parents are socialized from an early age to seek recognition where none exists, to assume their families' reputations determine their worth, and to internalize the message that their importance is determined by how well they can 'serve' their parents' needs. They also see a life in which love was rarely, if ever, unconditional.

This isn't to say that narcissistic violence survivors can't rise above their childhood conditioning; in truth, they can be stronger survivors and thrivers due to their resilience and how they turn their traumas into transformation. To unravel the traumas we've had to undergo as children, as well as to overcome any retraumatization as adults, it takes real inner work and courage. Understanding our relationship and behavioural patterns, as well as any negative self-talk that has developed as a result of the violence, can be transformative in debunking the myths and lies we've been fed about our worth and skill.

As the child of a narcissistic parent, I'm writing this list to explain how and why we can quickly become "trapped" in another cycle of violence that we're all too familiar with.

1. Love-bombing is a metaphor for our parents' undivided attention, which we might never have got.

Like narcissistic abusers in marriages, narcissistic parents pathologize and invalidate our feelings to the point that we are left speechless. We are not supposed to feel, so we either become repressed and numb, or we become rebellious children who "feel" too much, too soon. Our grief is not processed safely beginning in childhood, so our feelings become unbearable in either case.

Childhood experiences of not being heard, seen, loved, or validated can teach us to accept less while simultaneously demanding more. While everyone can be a target of love-bombing, a narcissist's undue attention to exploit us during the idealization process of a relationship can retraumatize survivors even further.

We can be more vulnerable to the love-bombing and idealization of a narcissist due to these past trauma experiences because we have more motivation to pursue the affirmation we didn't get in our previous experiences. When a toxic person love-bombs us and then devalues us, it reinforces those wounds while also inflicting new emotional injuries. However, this does not make the violence our fault; it just means that we have a greater amount of healing to do than survivors dealing with a narcissistic abuser for the first time.

2. **We've all experienced idealization when our parents wanted anything and devaluation when we were no longer needed.**

Narcissistic parents treat their children as trophies and objects— puppets who must do their bidding and represent them at all costs, even though they are perpetually unhappy with them. This cycle of idealization and devaluation tells us that love is insecure, scary, and ultimately unpredictable. It makes us nervous as if we're walking on eggshells for fear of offending someone. It even desensitizes us to verbal harassment and makes us tone-deaf later in life (Streep, 2016). While we can learn to recognize emotional and verbal violence, we would be less likely than someone who has had a stable childhood to recognize how harmful it can be or how unacceptable it is because it is sadly 'familiar' to us as the only version of love we have seen. As a result, we become "trauma bonded" to our abusive parents and more likely to bond with abusive spouses as adults (Carnes, 1997).

Our subconscious, which has been embedded with the habit of longing for our parents' approval—and that behavioural pattern has now been passed on to our new partner—feels oddly and masochistically at home with this sweet-and-mean loop. We learn to expect even less in decency and respect as we become accustomed to the crumbs of highly conditional love and acceptance. We might also shut out someone who has a tone or attitude that reminds us of our parents—some of this is hypervigilance, but most of it is self-protection and curiosity about the habits that have traumatized us the past.

By correcting their people-pleasing behaviours, doing essential boundary work, and replacing old narratives of unworthiness with empowering narratives about the sort of love and respect they deserve, children of narcissistic parents will re-sensitize themselves to the reality that violence is not a natural or healthy part of any relationship. In a healthy, protective environment, they can effectively 'reparent' themselves.

3. **We're used to being micromanaged and manipulated. Power, fear, and manipulation have been normalized in our culture as a means of intimacy rather than violence.**

The demands and personalities of their overbearing, manipulating parents begin to entangle narcissistic children. These parents are notorious for constantly invading their children's privacy and violating their boundaries. They work to erode the child's personality for him or her to become the ideal source of narcissistic supply. This entails using bullying, threats, and verbal, physical, or even sexual abuse to manipulate the child's interests, activities, desires, relationships, and even personality traits.

Children of narcissistic parents were given the blue pill of conformity as infants because they were never allowed to be autonomous. They haven't yet "awakened" to the fact that their people-pleasing tendencies can cause them to over-indulge in giving to people who don't deserve it. Fear is considered a natural part of a relationship. If we don't have it, we may feel strangely "bored" by the lack of adrenaline, dopamine, and oxytocin levels we're used to from our parents' occasional love bombing and scapegoating.

4. **Seeing the dynamics of one partner abusing the other causes us to imitate the positions as adults.**

It should come as no surprise that those who grew up in homes where domestic abuse was prevalent are much more likely to become victims or perpetrators themselves (UNICEF, 2006). When boys start dating, they are more likely to be abusive with their partners, and girls are more likely to become victims of that violence. Children who have experienced domestic violence can bully and display hostility against their peers, according to Liz Roberts, deputy CEO of Safe Horizon. This charity works with domestic violence victims in New York City.

It's important to remember, though, that not every abuser is an abuse victim, and not every abuse victim becomes an abuser. Abuse is always a decision made by another. Because of their diminished empathy, full-fledged narcissists can find it difficult or impossible to adapt, but survivors of violence may evolve and learn from their trauma.

Children with narcissistic parents, whether male or female, are at a higher risk of being narcissistically manipulated or being narcissistic themselves, in my opinion. As we grow up, we can come to identify with the victim parent or even develop "fleas" of narcissistic tendencies that we must learn from during our healing process.

5. We learn to equate being valued as an entity.

You were told as a child of a narcissistic parent or parents that you were not necessarily valuable but that your value was determined by what you could do for the narcissistic parent and how obedient you were. In families with narcissistic parent, the focus on appearance, rank, and prestige is at an all-time high. You were undoubtedly part of a family that was 'presented' in the best possible light, with violence taking place behind closed doors, due to the narcissistic parent's grandiosity, false mask, and desire to be the best.

You may have witnessed the horrible dynamics of one parent verbally or physically abusing the other, been exposed to the violence and neglect yourself, and/or witnessed both parents working together to undercut you and your siblings. You were almost certainly disciplined if you dared to challenge the flawless false picture or did something to speak out against the violence. The emotional and psychological abuse that children of abusive parents face when they defy the family's expectations and values can be devastating, affecting their self-esteem, agency, and trust in themselves for the rest of their lives. For a young child, existing solely to protect someone else's image is a very restricting experience. It's terrifying to be told that you're here to serve someone else.

Being a trophy boyfriend, girlfriend, wife, or husband could seem flattering at first because being a prize as a child felt like a seal of approval—and the only source of "true" affection and recognition from your parents.

6. If we were scapegoated as children, we would experience toxic guilt and a persistent sense of

unworthiness, which will keep us from realizing we deserve better.

This is referred to as "toxic guilt" by Pete Walker (2013). It's a symptom of Complex PTSD, which often occurs as a result of selfish violence. When we become entangled with a narcissist who may or may not be the spitting image of one or both of our parents, we return to the feelings of powerlessness and guilt that have plagued us since we were children.

A relationship with a toxic narcissist in adulthood is likely to cause and cement the feeling of never being quite enough and despised for simply existing. What do you think happens if we keep reiterating the toxic shame? We end up feeling insufficient all over again, and we become traumatized by our abuser, who represents the people we failed to please as children. Although the rational, reasoning part of our brain tells us to flee, our subconscious instincts lead us straight to the attacker, who looks and acts eerily like the people we relied on for survival.

7. **We have a far higher pain tolerance than people who have never been abused; we're more desensitized to toxicity and are more likely to hang on even when things are bad.**

Contempt is considered a part of marriage and 'normal' in a relationship when you are raised by a narcissist or two narcissistic parents. When we 'disobey' and threaten the parent's unreasonable sense of superiority, we are treated well only when required and then treated with disdain and frightening narcissistic anger (Goulston, 2012). A narcissistic parent's condescension, disdain, and resentment against their children are not only hurtful, but it also retrains the mind to embrace violence as the new standard.

Writer Peg Streep (2016) claims that after witnessing childhood violence, we become "tone-deaf" to verbal abuse, desensitized to toxic experiences to the point of not even processing it as abuse in her article "Why Unloved Daughters Fall For Narcissists." The violence may deeply hurt us, but we may respond to it differently than those who have grown up in healthier homes without abuse and can better recognize it as a deal-breaker.

To survive in such a hostile environment, we can establish what Patrick Carnes (2013) refers to as "betrayal bonds" or "trauma bonds," which are similar to Stockholm Syndrome. This trauma bonding can also happen in adulthood with an abuser, which is much more dangerous for the victim who is still weak. Indeed, according to Dr Martin Teicher (2006), growing evidence suggests that verbal violence in childhood can alter brain wiring, raising the risk of anxiety and suicidal ideation in adulthood. There have been corresponding research that confirms that parental verbal abuse can result in brain changes.

Being raised by a narcissistic parent can physically alter our brain, rendering us a completely different individual than we were before the trauma. The hippocampus, amygdala, corpus callosum, and frontal cortex are all brain regions affected by trauma. Furthermore, trauma causes changes in key stress-related neural networks, such as the HPA axis—chronic activation wears out parts of the body, resulting in hippocampal/limbic defects in infants. Trauma has changed how our brain handles new trauma, making it difficult for us to feel strong enough to escape another abusive situation without the proper help. When we are in constant fight, flight, freeze, or fawn mode, we are unlikely to be able to focus our resources on how to develop a healthy emotional detachment from the situation—if we are abandoned, particularly by a toxic partner who resembles a parental figure, it feels like death to our brain, and we can feel the need to find every way possible to avoid the reduction.

8. **We were accustomed to conditional encouragement because we were never recognized or praised for our successes unless they benefited our parents.**

Parents who are narcissistic teach their children that they must be perfect and good but that they should never be praised for it or feel "enough." Narcissists are experts at shifting the goalposts so that nothing their victims do ever seems to be enough. We are no exception to this law as survivors of childhood violence. Our achievements are seldom recognized unless they fulfil predetermined expectations for "what seems best to society" or validate the narcissistic parent's grandiose delusions. Our controlling parent is never really proud of us until he or she can take credit for our accomplishments. Some narcissistic parents may envy or look down on their children's success, particularly if that success allows them to become self-sufficient and independent of their parents, outside of their sphere of power and control.

It's not uncommon for these parents to try to sabotage their children's success and happiness if it gets in the way of their grandiose self-image, their ideas of what "happiness" might entail (usually whatever makes them look good rather than what makes their children feel good), or their need to micromanage and control every aspect of their children's lives.

In the twisted mind of the narcissistic parent, it would be preferable if their children did not exist, rather than being unwilling to do their bidding and 'perform' the identity that the parent desires their children to uphold or accomplish the exact goals they want. Even if they were ideal daughters or sons, the goalposts would move once more. That is why the expression "Your parents must be so proud" elicits a cringe and a ride down trauma memory lane for children with narcissistic parents.

When you say that, what are we thinking?

"No matter what I do, my parents are rarely proud of me. It was never enough for them. Regardless of what they did, I mostly raised myself and achieved this."

Please understand that, though well-intentioned, these platitudes can be triggering for survivors of childhood violence or trauma, as we were never accepted or cherished unconditionally by our parents, or at the very least, one of our parents. As a result, children of narcissistic parents yearn for the optimistic attention that only a narcissist can appear to offer—they yearn for the excessive attention that only a narcissist can provide. The children of narcissists may be duped into thinking that they've finally found a source of unconditional support while dating a narcissistic abuser. This may feel addictive to the children of narcissists who may be duped into thinking that they've finally found a source of unconditional support. But what they're seeing is a conditional period of encouragement that lasts only as long as the narcissist's idealization phase.

9. **Your manipulative parent or parents could have instilled in you a "fixer" mentality.**

Children of narcissists may become accustomed to walking on eggshells or even acting as primary caregivers for their parents at a young age if they have an abusive, rageful parent or parents.

Since narcissists may have drug abuse problems in addition to their personality disorders, there is sometimes a role reversal. This is particularly true if either or both parents are abusers of any kind. If we build a "fixer" or "codependent" (a controversial concept in the survivor community) mentality toward an abuser, we're more likely to bring the desire to serve or help those in need into our future relationships.

It's important to note that feeling empathy, compassion, and a desire to support others is perfectly normal. None of these characteristics should be eliminated, even though they make us more vulnerable to predators who seek to take advantage of them. Excessively putting someone else's desires ahead of your own, on the other hand, is a prescription for frustration and a lack of satisfaction in the long run. The phrases "Sorry," "Hope I'm not troubling you," and "I can do that for you, no worries" are all too familiar to children of narcissists. 365 days a year. It can be difficult for us to recognize that our own needs are important and that we often need to put our own needs ahead of the desires of others.

10. You're attempting to transform a toxic individual into the family you never had, when in fact, they are identical to the family you did have.

Maslow's pyramid and the hierarchy of needs were disrupted by abusive parents, according to integrative psychotherapist Maxine Harley (2016). The experience of having a narcissistic parent present distorts our desire for identity, a safe place, and a house. What may seem healthy to a child raised in a normal home may seem unusual and foreign to a child raised in an abusive home. Our haven might sound like it's in the arms of another narcissist, similar to the one or ones who raised us. That is why, rather than relying on our partner as a parent (whether harmful or not), it is important to "re-parent" ourselves, soothe ourselves, and be gentle with ourselves as if we were our own children, recognizing

75

that we will always have ourselves as a guiding light of support. Only after we've re-parented ourselves and grieved the loss of our childhood can we be completely accepting and open to obtaining a spouse who will help and love us with the same zeal as we do when we're in need.

The consequences of growing up with a narcissist are nuanced and varied, depending on the degree of trauma encountered, the child's willingness to isolate and live a life apart from his or her parents, and their coping tools. However, after surveying hundreds of survivors and speaking with thousands throughout my life, I've discovered that we share many commonalities that prevent us from living the happy, fulfilling lives we deserve. Consider the following scenario:

- *We feel undeserving and unworthy of good fortune when things are going well.* We sabotage our own happiness and achievement because we've been taught to believe we don't deserve it. I recall a thoughtful reader congratulating me on a recent life-changing experience I documented on social media—it was a post about realizing a long-held ambition. She said something extraordinary to me that I will never forget. "You deserve anything and more," she said.

- *You are deserving of all of this and more.* Even though she was an unknown outsider, she said something that I had never heard from my own parents. How many of us need to hear these terms as narcissistic violence survivors? Those were some of the most powerful words a survivor, particularly one who had experienced childhood narcissistic violence, could hear. What's more, you know what? That is what we all need to remind ourselves of if something positive occurs. "I really believe I am deserving of this. I don't have to feel bad for succeeding, working hard, achieving my goals, being my own guy, or being content. I am deserving of all of this and more. I believe that. And I don't have to battle the abundance that is coming my way. I am deserving of prosperity and happiness."

Our greatest challenge is to recognize and rejoice in our worthiness. We are, in fact, just as deserving as anyone who had a typical happy childhood. In reality, I'd wager that we deserve ten times the love and compassion that those who haven't had a traumatic childhood get because we need it so much more. We must literally "love-bomb" ourselves—but not in the fake, superficial way that the narcissistic abuser or parent did if they wanted anything from us. In a genuine way that respects our true selves, faults, gifts, triumphs, and fears. We aren't flawless, but we are lovable and deserving of love.

- *We are apprehensive about taking up space and requesting what we want.* We're embarrassed to the point of being apologetic. Children of narcissistic parents learn to say sorry for having simple desires and needs, as I previously mentioned. I've been working on my limits for years, and I'm still struggling to break this habit! We can find ourselves attempting to appease others while asking for something, qualifying our desires with "No worries if you can't," or sacrificing our limits out of fear of upsetting others. We may also physically manifest this by overeating or undereating to take up less physical space or hiding under extra weight because we don't want to be noticed.

- *We give those who don't deserve it a second, third, and hundredth chance.* While I am not a golden child, I have seen both golden children and scapegoats continue to bond with manipulative parents because they refuse to believe there is little hope for a stable and authentic relationship. We are taught from a young age that we must accept, change, adapt, and withstand as much as humanly possible when we are subjected to violence. Consequently, we take the behaviour into adulthood and continue to give people a million chances who promise to improve but never do. Perhaps we expect that if our spouses change, our parents will change as well. But what we need to alter are our patterns of saying yes when we really need to say no, as well as our patterns of sticking to our guns and avoiding toxicity wherever possible.

- *We discover that if we want to be deemed worthy, we must be the strongest.* We internalize the notion that there is always someone better, and you must beat them—starting with your own siblings—as children of narcissistic parents. Children of abusive parents often pit their siblings against one another in a competition for the attention and devotion they have often craved but never earned. Narcissistic parents are notorious for pitting their children against one another to compare, demean, and feed their own sense of power and influence over their children.

Typically, there is a golden child and a scapegoat, but the roles may be reversed depending on the narcissistic parent's agenda (McBride, 2011). Scapegoated rebel children are always truth-seekers and want an authentic relationship with their family members. Still, they don't speak up about the bullying they face when they don't live up to their parents' unrealistic standards. The golden child, on the other hand, is always praised as the 'golden norm,' but this can easily deteriorate if the golden child exercises his or her agency and does something that is beyond the parent's control. We are told from a young age that we will never be good enough, that we must constantly compare ourselves to others, and that we must never recognize our own intrinsic worth and importance. We learn as adults that we don't have to compete with others to be deserving or valuable, and we don't have to be the best at all. Cultivating a sense of unconditional self-love, as well as an appreciation for our special talents and abilities, will help counteract these negative internalizations from violence and replace them with a healthy sense of confidence and self-sufficiency.

- ***We choose partners and friends who aren't happy or who aren't positive in a good way.*** We choose those who may seem overly supportive at first, only to be subjected to envious criticism, diminution of our performance, and sabotage later on. This is because a part of us is uncomfortable with the thought of someone fully embracing us. We have no idea what it's like to have a group of people who are really there for us. We only know conditional support, which is support provided in exchange for doing anything to make our parents look good. Similarly, we are conditioned to make our partners look good when they need it, but not to make them feel good for the things that make us a "trophy" in their eyes.

- ***A good sense of safety and positive self-esteem should have been cultivated, there is a gap and an emptiness.*** In its place is a huge vacuum that is often filled with toxic guilt that does not belong to us or any innocent child. It was never ours in the first place. It was projected onto us by those who were supposed to raise, care for, and unconditionally love us. Survivors must know that it takes a lot of inner effort, self-parenting, and clinical resources to learn how to fill these holes safely and nourishing way, in a way that respectfully helps us to parent ourselves, to alleviate feelings of toxic guilt and self-blame. There may be no substitute for a parent's affection or attention, but that does not rule out the possibility of healing.

Please understand that if you were traumatized or re-traumatized as a child of a narcissistic parent or parents, it was not your fault. You can break your habits by healing some of your subconscious wounding and convictions, which often begins with the most powerful conviction, "I am not enough." This might include using healing modalities that address the mind, body, and spirit to smash some of the subconscious, self-defeating attitudes and rituals that have been holding you back. "Healing The Narcissistic Addiction" and "Healing Invisible Battle Wounds," two of my posts, provide more detail on the various healing modalities available to complex trauma survivors.

It's important to remember that you will recover at your rate throughout this period. To begin to recover, we must re-parent, process the pain of not having a caring parent, and work through the complex feelings that can occur when we have No Contact or Low Contact with our parents. Working with a therapist who is familiar with PTSD and Complex PTSD, somatic practices like yoga and Reiki, hypnosis, meditation, positive affirmations, and, most importantly, a break from relationships that allows you to explore your core beliefs without the risk of reinforcing them by being with someone can all help. After being with a narcissistic partner, some people find the love of their lives, while others find themselves back in the circle, tortured once more. That is why, for survivors of this type of violence, taking a break from relationships can be extremely beneficial and necessary to continue living the dream of the former without risking falling back into the latter.

We gain the ability to affirm our own feelings as adults and understand that what we feel, and have felt all along, is completely real. As children and teenagers, we learn how to process our feelings, trauma, and the sorrow of being unloved. We learn that we should separate from our abusive parents by Low Contact (minimal contact only when necessary) or No Contact at all. We try to distinguish ourselves from the identity erosion that happened during our childhoods by using our organization. We learn to distinguish between our own burgeoning faith and the narcissistic parent's negative assumptions regarding us. Most importantly, we learn that believing in ourselves and welcoming positive things into our lives is perfectly acceptable. We learn that we are worthy of all positive in life.

It's important to note that as children of narcissistic parents, we inherit our wounds, but that these wounds can also serve as portals to deeper, more meaningful healing. We don't have to leave our wounds on the next generation; instead, we can use them to nurture and affirm future generations. We have choices in how we can use this trauma to help us flourish rather than destroy ourselves. These wounds will not heal if they are not addressed or if we fail to be awake; at the same time, our healing period will be special, and we will not be able to equate our path to others'. Self-awareness and humility are more important than ever.

We must learn to defend ourselves from more violence as children of abusive parents and create a strategy to properly participate in self-care. When it comes to manipulative, poisonous, and abusive parents, lies about parents always being caring and having our best interests at heart just do not cut it. These parents lack empathy and will just 'hoover' you back when they need to use you as a source of narcissistic supply. We must encourage ourselves to mourn the loss of our childhood and acknowledge the reality that while our parents might not have loved us or desired the best for us, we can 'reparent' ourselves in the best ways we know how—through empathy, compassion, self-acceptance, and self-love. Make no mistake: believing that you never deserved this love as a child of a narcissistic parent is probably the biggest lie of all.

5 Self-Care Tips for Survivors of Abuse and Trauma

Being a trauma survivor is a difficult road to travel, but it is also a rewarding one. Trauma catalyzes for us to learn how to properly participate in self-care and exposes us to a plethora of healing and expression modalities, allowing us to change our crisis. Most importantly, it allows us to interact with other survivors who have been through similar experiences. Even outside of the therapy room, we seem to find the most healing in these validating groups. Here are some pointers I've learned over the years that can help those who have experienced trauma or violence on their road to recovery.

1. **Positive Affirmations**

We must literally reprogram our brain and minimize the negative, damaging automatic thoughts that can occur in our day-to-day lives in order to reprogram our subconscious mind, which has certainly been influenced by the violent words and acts we've experienced.

These thoughts encourage self-destructive behaviour and prevent us from fully accepting the strength and agency we have to restore our lives. Many of these thoughts are the voices of our abusers and bullies, who continue to torment us even after the violence has stopped. When we've been abused or bullied in some way, we continue to punish ourselves with the voice of the "inner critic," according to trauma therapist Pete Walker.

Positive affirmations, which I use on a regular basis, are the most effective way I've reprogrammed my own inner vital speech. There are affirmations that can be customized to your specific wounds and insecurities. For example, if your abuser has tried to instil in you a sense of shame regarding your appearance, a constructive reinforcement will gently disrupt the habit of ruminating on those harsh remarks by replacing the toxic thinking with a loving one. Whenever the negative thought or emotion associated with the thought arises, a self-sabotaging thought about your appearance transforms into, "I am beautiful, inside and out."

Record all of your positive affirmations on tape or in a voice recording app and listen to them every day. Hearing your own voice say these affirmations every day—"I love myself," "I am valuable," "I am worthy," "I am beautiful"—is a powerful way to rewrite the story that bullies have written for you and to get rid of the browbeating bully within your head.

2. Heal your mind by healing your body.

Trauma lives in our bodies as well as our brains, according to trauma specialist Dr Bessel van der Kolk, author of The Body Keeps the Score. In order to overcome the paralysis that follows trauma, leaving us feeling numb and frozen, it's critical that we find at least one kind of physical outlet for the intense emotions of sorrow, anger, and hurt we're bound to feel in the aftermath of violence and trauma.

Kickboxing, meditation, dance fitness, and running are some of my favourite activities to do when listening to empowering music or optimistic affirmations. Do something you're enthusiastic about and enjoy. Don't push your body into things it doesn't want to do or exhaust yourself. Physical activity should be viewed as a form of self-care rather than self-destruction.

3. Take a deep breath

Mindful breathing exercises and meditation are particularly beneficial for violence survivors who deal with PTSD or complicated PTSD symptoms, according to therapist Pete Walker (2013), in controlling our battle, flight, freeze, or fawn reactions to memories and ruminating thoughts.

Taking five minutes or an hour to observe our breath can be extremely beneficial in calming our feelings and nonjudgmentally discussing our painful causes. Furthermore, meditation rewires our brain, allowing us to approach any maladaptive responses that may hold us stuck in the traumatic event with mindfulness. If you have never meditated before and want to give it a shot, I highly recommend the app Stop, Breathe, and Think, which is suitable for people of all ages.

4. Transform your pain into something creative.

Art therapy is particularly beneficial to PTSD patients because it allows them to discover new ways of expressing themselves that enable them to create rather than self-destruct. Trauma may influence Broca's region of the brain, which deals with language, according to van der Kolk. It can shut down this part of the brain, preventing us from expressing what is going on.

Since trauma and the dissociation that comes with it are difficult to put into words, allowing us to articulate the trauma in a bodily way is critical. When we are dissociated from a traumatic experience, our brain protects us by giving us an outsider view on the event, disconnecting us from our identity, emotions, feelings, and memories associated with the trauma.

A traumatic experience is also "split" in the brain to make it easier to process (Kalsched, 2013). Since trauma can cause us to lose touch with our minds and bodies through derealization, depersonalization and even amnesia, art can help us reintegrate the trauma in places where we were previously disconnected. According to Andrea Schneider, LCSW, expressive arts will help us "master the trauma" we've been through.

It's essential to release the trauma in alternative ways that engage both our mind and body, whether it's writing, painting, drawing, making music, or doing arts and crafts. When we make something, we have the choice of sharing it with the rest of the world—whether it's a beautiful painting or a book—turning our suffering into inspiration can be a life-changing experience for both ourselves and others.

5. Seeking help

Seeking help does not make you vulnerable or weak, contrary to common belief. To be willing to seek support and be open to receiving it is, in reality, a clear acknowledgement of your strength. It can be very healing and cathartic to share your experience with other survivors. If you are suffering from the effects of trauma, I strongly advise you to seek out a professional mental health professional who specializes in trauma and is familiar with its symptoms, as well as a support network of fellow survivors.

Utilizing the support of a mental health professional in the process will help you address the trauma causes in a healthy environment. It's important to find a validating, trauma-informed counsellor who will meet your needs and gently direct you to the right treatment for your symptoms and triggers. Some trauma survivors benefit from EMDR therapy, which allows them to process their trauma without re-traumatizing themselves. However, depending on the individual symptoms, the severity of the trauma, and the amount of time a person has been traumatized, a treatment that works for one survivor can not work for another. Be sure to discuss which form of counselling is best for you with your mental health provider.

Make sure you're gentle to yourself when you're recovering from trauma and violence. Many trauma survivors are plagued by toxic guilt and self-blame. We must be gentle with ourselves in this journey, that we recognize that we are doing our best and that we ask ourselves every day, in every situation, "What would be the most caring thing I can do for myself at this moment?" Learning and healing have no time limits; all we have is the chance to turn our adversity into triumph, our powerlessness into power, one small step at a time.

CHAPTER SIX
WHAT DOES IT TAKE TO WORK IN A NARCISSISTIC ORGANIZATION?

Top management dedication is needed to sustain progress. The atmosphere of the company would not improve without the active intervention of the senior team. Only highly visible, new actions from the top will lead the company away from narcissistic practices.

Functioning inside the System

The only way for a business to avoid a narcissistic culture is for reform to start at the top and work its way down. Without the encouragement and power of top management, any effort to make such a drastic and significant shift is doomed to fail.

Organizational improvement isn't always necessary. What do you do when top management engages in narcissistic behaviour? Do you want to go? Attempt to alter the company on your own? Neither of these options is usually an option. You must learn to work inside a narcissistic environment without being broken in these situations. In this chapter, we'll look at how to function in a narcissistic culture without losing your sanity or your ethics.

Working with a narcissistic boss is certainly challenging. However, it is possible. Learning to work with the narcissist begins with understanding the narcissistic style and its roots. You may also take some concrete steps to help neutralize the narcissistic atmosphere and maintain a positive, efficient working relationship.

Know Yourself

Looking at yourself is the first step of learning how to deal with a narcissist. "Know yourself," as the old adage goes, has never been more real. Do I know who I am? Isn't narcissism, however, his issue? As strange as it might seem, the first step in working with a narcissist is to have a clear and relaxed understanding of yourself. More precisely, you must discuss your requirements and desires to meet them. After all, how you react to a narcissist accounts for half of your working relationship.

You won't be able to explain why you respond to the narcissist the way you do if you don't understand your own needs. You can only understand others to the extent that you understand yourself.

You Can't Change the Narcissists

Accepting that you can't alter the narcissist is just as crucial as accepting yourself. A narcissist's long-standing attitude would not improve without intense therapy or major self-discovery. Once a narcissist has risen to the level of management, he has received years of support for his narcissistic actions. Behaviours that have a long history, are intricately linked to his self-esteem, and have been used successfully for years are difficult to alter. To be effective, this type of transition necessitates a long and painful period of hard work. The narcissist must make the decision to improve on his own, and no one can make that decision for him.

Bringing up the need for reform isn't going to help; in fact, it's going to make things worse. After all, his narcissistic tendencies have served him well throughout his life; why should he change now?

The true irony of narcissism is that most people seek support after something has gone wrong. Since the narcissistic cycle is so tenacious, it normally takes the possibility of utter personal collapse to motivate shift. That assistance often necessitates a lengthy process of re-framing one's entire life. Only the narcissist has the ability to do this for himself. Accepting the narcissist as he is is the only option if you can't change him. The relationship's success hinges on your willingness to accept his needs for what they are and function within those constraints. Any relationship success is contingent on how you act before the change occurs.

What Are Your Personal Needs?

The narcissist's motives can be divided into two categories: a powerful desire for dominance and a desire for acknowledgement. Anything he does is overshadowed by these two types of needs. It's good to think about yourself in terms of these two types of needs if you want to figure out how to deal with a narcissist. In this relationship, what needs are you trying to meet? What inspires you? Examine your own desires for dominance and affirmation, and consider how you may be satisfying them in your relationship with the narcissist. Since business relationships are often the agents we use to meet our needs, it is critical that you recognize what you require from the narcissist.

The Three "Cs"

You'll notice that the majority of problems in your partnership with a narcissist arise because you're both trying to meet the same desires, perhaps with the same methods. The following are the three most common issues that arise when this occurs:

1. *Competition.* When two people are attempting to achieve the same objective, one must succeed, and the other must fail, and both must continually compare their results to the others in order to know where they stand. In a partnership, competition undermines cooperation, coordination, and mutual assistance.
2. *Conflict.* Conflict arises when both sides deliberately work to disrupt, outsmart, and dominate the other in order to gain power, just like two nations battling for the same territory. When jurisdictions overlap or have ambiguous borders, disagreements over who is in charge and who reports to whom are unavoidable.
3. **Compatibility.** Compatibility is the third point to consider. When one group is primarily focused on satisfying internal motivations, and the other is primarily focused on extrinsic motivations, incompatibility arises. Their respective actions become a puzzle to each other, causing utter befuddlement. In its most serious, neither party comprehends the motives for the other's behaviour.

The sections that follow take a closer look at all three of these, as well as some methods for dealing with them when they arise. It's important to remember that none of these will fully solve the problem, but they will assist you in maintaining your sanity and your work.

COMPETITION

When both people want to be recognized, it can be a source of conflict in a business partnership. Competition is the result of two people attempting to achieve the same goal and receiving credit for it.

Suggestions for Managing Competition

1. Create a simple division of labour. Both parties should be aware of the activities they are responsible for completing, with as little overlap as possible.
2. Demonstrate how your performance will assist the other group in achieving their goals. To put it another way, make it clear to the other person that you aren't involved in "stealing their thunder," but rather in assisting them in making even more noise.
3. Don't be a glutton for punishment. Share the spotlight with the other person when it's necessary. Enable them to get the credit they are due.
4. If all else fails, look for another project that can satisfy your need for accomplishment and recognition.

CONFLICT

When both parties have a strong desire for dominance, it can trigger problems in business relationships, much like the desire for recognition.

Suggestions for Conflict Resolution Suggestions

1. Establish a clear line of responsibility between the two parties. Everyone should have his own control territory with the least amount of overlap as possible.
2. Maintain the highest degree of consensus in your discussions. Disagreement is more likely to arise when addressing specifics rather than general goals.
3. When a manager and an employee are at odds, the employee should convince the boss that he agrees with the broader goals and ask to be in charge of a smaller area within those objectives.
4. If all else fails, look for another project with clearly specified obligations that will satisfy the need for power.

COMPATIBILITY

The "locus of motivation" is one of the most reliable personality tests. There are two potential outcomes for the locus of motivation: intrinsic or extrinsic. People who have an inherent locus of motivation are energized by their own internal beliefs and desires. They participate in activities because they like them or because they make them feel comfortable. Persons with an extrinsic locus of motivation, on the other hand, are motivated by external incentives and recognition. As you would expect, the narcissist has an extrinsic locus of motivation.

Compatibility issues may arise when two people have polar opposite motivation loci, one high extrinsic and the other high intrinsic. Compatibility is described as one's ability to comprehend another's motivations for acting the way they do. While two people who are compatible can not agree on everything, they understand each other's motives. Two incompatible individuals, on the other hand, find each other's actions perplexing and unpredictable. Understanding another person's actions is crucial to the concept of compatibility.

Extrinsic motivation is when an individual wants to meet his needs by obtaining external incentives. Increases in pay, popularity, increased exposure, and other variables that are visible to those around him guide his actions. He participates in events that give out external incentives as a re-suit. An individual with high intrinsic motivation seeks to meet his needs by doing what feels good, is compatible with his beliefs, and aids in the development of his own competence. As a result, he engages in actions that have inherent consequences for him. As you would expect, the activities that these two people engage in are often very different.

RESISTANCE

Finally, resistance is a roadblock that most people face while attempting to work with a narcissist. When I consult with a client on how to develop a narcissistic relationship, they invariably say things like, "However, you are unaware of so and so. Nothing I do will have any effect. All must be under his full control!" This is valid in some instances. Those pessimistic remarks, on the other hand, are often made by someone who is struggling to fulfil their own strength or success needs.

They have frequently made significant sacrifices to meet the narcissist's needs and now find themselves unable to compromise except in the tiniest of ways. They can be much more dogmatic in forcing their desires on the relationship than the narcissist in certain cases. The frustration of having to meet someone else's needs when your own go unmet can lead to a heavy-handed willingness to turn the tables in your favour, as well as a deep opposition to something that accommodates the narcissist in any way. Resistance will keep you from seeing potential options, which can lead to the end of an already shaky partnership.

Working with a narcissist necessitates patience, empathy, and a wealth of self-awareness. Compromise and careful negotiation are needed for relationship success. To make matters even more complicated, the relationship's resentment, frustration, and resistance will serve to further ruin it if not handled properly. Despite this, having a happy, fruitful relationship with a narcissist is possible. Finding ways to meet your own needs that aren't incompatible with his will help you make the relationship work. It is the only safe way to function together in the absence of drastic change.

CHAPTER SEVEN
STAGES OF RECOVERY FROM A
NARCISSISTIC ABUSE

Recovery is not a straight line. It could be all of us. You'll take forward and backward steps, questioning and blaming yourself. It's possible that you'll fall flat on your stomach. Remember that you've been belittled and dismissed in your most intimate relationships. It's likely that you're used to being white and anted. Prevarication and rumination can also cause you to white ant yourself. Nobody needs to be abused. All need to be acknowledged and to experience real intimacy in their relationships.

SURPRISE AND DENIAL

"I am not in love with a narcissist. They genuinely care for me, despite my shortcomings. Maybe if I just try harder, they'll give me the love and attention I deserve..."

You'll be unable to admit to yourself that your partner is a narcissist at first. After all, you've been dating for quite some time. They're very affectionate or were when they first met. However, things are a little different now because, yeah, they're busy. They make an effort. If they can't keep the romance alive, it's not their fault. Every relationship has its ups and downs. That's perfectly natural. They aren't flawless, and you aren't either. However, some nagging questions remain.

PAIN & RESPONSIBILITY

You'll blame yourself for getting involved with someone so deceitful and dishonest as you learn to recognize and appreciate narcissistic characteristics in your spouse. You'll feel the pain of putting too much effort into trying to make a narcissistic relationship function. You've always given in to their thoughts, wishes, and desires. You've sacrificed too much to be with them.

"Did I really miss those warning signs? How could I have made such a blunder? I was always attempting to satisfy them. I've squandered too much passion, affection, and time on someone who isn't really interested in me. Perhaps I'll never be able to get what I want from this guy. I just wanted to believe in the good guys. I'm embarrassed and guilty for allowing myself to be seduced and put up with too much."

RAGE AND BARGAINING

"I'm furious at my husband for deceiving, manipulating, and seducing me. But if I just put in a little more effort, maybe they'll improve. I'll get the love I deserve if I keep sacrificing my own desires for theirs."

You will become enraged as your journey progresses. That is a good thing. However, you may find yourself reverting to hope and attempting to persuade the narcissist to alter. Remember that narcissists will not improve unless there is a benefit to them or they reach a breaking point. You could spend a lot of time and effort waiting for them to grasp your point of view. Narcissists have a poor capacity to empathize and would turn the conversation around and make it about them. They might also go so far as to make themselves appear to be the victim.

LONELINESS, REFLECTION, AND DEPRESSION

"I've always been truthful, loving, and caring. I've even been betrayed. I have the impression that I would never find the right person for me. They took advantage of my insecurity because I felt I loved my partner. They've left me feeling drained. They never loved me, I realize now. I've been duped. I have a hard time trusting others. Will I ever meet someone who is concerned about my well-being? "What if I fall into yet another toxic relationship?"

Not only must you reckon with and appreciate your partner's shortcomings, but you must also face the difficulty of processing challenging emotions. Therapy will assist you in growing and learning. It will help you to gradually and effectively integrate your trauma. This is one of the most crucial steps, and I strongly advise you not to go through it alone.

THE UPWARD TURN

"There is reason to be hopeful. I have caring friends who have supported me during this journey of self-discovery. There are those who aren't really looking out for themselves. I am deserving of love, and I will surround myself with people who genuinely care."

You will begin to feel better after you have liberated yourself and accepted the truth of your partner's narcissism. You could even reach a point where you're ready to start dating again. When you realize that not everyone is like your ex, optimism returns. Cleaning up your relationship house will make you feel better about your relationships. Get rid of people and relationships where you aren't taken into account or understood. Payers, freeloaders, energy vampires, and invalidators should all be thrown out. Bring together those who really care and are able to participate in mutually beneficial relationships.

RECONSTRUCTION AND WORKING THROUGH THE PROBLEM

"I need to let go in order to heal my heart and take the risk of relating again. I need to think about my own insecurity and willingness to work with the narcissist. I am a self-aware person who accepts responsibility for my conduct, but I do not absolve the narcissist."

Accept that you will never be able to influence the narcissist and that you are not to blame for their actions or mental bankruptcy. Even though it was not your fault, you should think about how you got caught and why you put up with the violence. Are you more vulnerable to narcissists' predations? Was there a narcissist in your extended family? Is your sense of self-worth shattered?

HOPE AND ACCEPTANCE

"Yes, I made a blunder. Everyone has their own set of circumstances. Maybe I'll be able to restore and re-learn to trust. Maybe I'll be able to have mutual relationships in which I'm respected and cherished. I'll strengthen my communication and assertiveness skills, as well as my self-awareness, so I don't have to negate myself again."

Develop the abilities you'll need to defend yourself. Develop self-awareness so that you can recognize and appreciate your own needs and desires. Self-compassion and imagination will aid in reflection and development.

It can be a long and difficult journey. Failure and repair are also necessary parts of the operation. But, with luck, you'll keep stumbling in the right direction toward self-awareness, self-compassion, and true healing. The final stage of post-traumatic development is reconnecting with your true self.

CHAPTER EIGHT
THE TREATMENT AND MANAGEMENT OF NARCISSISM

How can you cope with a narcissist and handle the disease now that you know some typical narcissistic characteristics? Long-term outpatient treatment is the most effective way to treat narcissism in the long run. There are no medications known for narcissism. However, as we've seen, narcissism is a psychological issue, and as with all psychological issues, there are therapies available via a subscription with a licensed psychologist.

In an ideal world, narcissism will be treated with medication and psychotherapy, specifically psychoanalytic psychotherapy. This isn't to say that there aren't other approaches to its management and care. Many psychotherapists recommend family groups, couples therapy, and cognitive behavioural therapy because of the close connection to family issues.

A psychotherapist may also use concentrated short-term psychotherapy to help a client. As I previously said, there is no all-encompassing treatment for NPD (narcissistic personality disorder). The psychotherapist can choose to prescribe psychotropic medication to treat anxiety, impulsivity, depression, and a variety of other psychologically associated mood disorders at his or her discretion.

In most cases, outpatient care is the safest option. In cases where the narcissist poses a risk to himself or others, the psychotherapist may recommend inpatient care. Inpatient treatments are brief since a lengthy stay in the hospital jeopardizes the healing process. What do you mean by that? Longer hospital stays will expose the narcissist to all of the emotions he has been attempting to suppress until he develops the necessary coping mechanisms when undergoing treatment. Only enough time should be allowed for mood stabilization or proper medication dosage during an inpatient procedure.

There is no one-size-fits-all approach to treating narcissism; if you suspect you are dealing with a narcissist, the safest course of action is to seek diagnosis and care from a psychotherapist. With this in mind, a few aspects are thought to make it easier for anyone to identify with a suspected narcissist.

Managing anyone with narcissistic traits can take a lot of creativity, empathy, and grit, as well as an understanding of their characteristics so that you can take advantage of their sense of self-importance to deal with them.

- First, keep in mind that narcissists like being associated with dominance, so keep that in mind if you're at work. Maintain a safe distance. Request respect if you are superior to him. Demonstrate to them that you can quickly report them to the firm's management with only one phone call, and make sure to imply that everybody in top management knows your name and vice versa.
- Narcissists are not known for being team players. If you're working on a team project, pick the people who work well together and give the narcissist a solo project. If you don't have a solo project, but the narcissist in a group of people who are his equals and peers, or who he admires. The narcissist will often ask for special favours because they believe they are superior or unique. This is a privilege you

should not offer him. Follow the law. Don't make an exception for him or give in to their unreasonable requests.

- As we previously said, narcissists are still chasing glory. If a narcissist approaches you to claim credit for a good project you've completed, move up and refuse to let him take all the credit.

BREAKING THE BIOCHEMICAL BOND AND ADDICTION TO THE NARCISSIST

To counteract the biochemical ties we've mentioned, we must accept that when we cut communication with the narcissist, we will eventually experience withdrawal. This means dealing with withdrawal from elevated oxytocin levels, dopamine, adrenaline, and even cortisol spikes that our bodies have grown used to. There are healthier ways to satisfy these desires without involving the narcissist. Here are some natural ways to improve your feel-good hormones and replace your narcissistic addiction with positive activities.

Oxytocin production should be increased.

No Contact or Low Contact is needed to begin weaning off the oxytocin bond's effects, but it will inevitably be accompanied by cravings to reconnect with the narcissistic partner. Rather than succumbing to the urge to reconnect, replace it with healthy relationships. Such instances are as follows:

Increase physical contact

Cuddling a cute animal or a caring friend or family member releases oxytocin; research indicates that cuddling with a dog raises oxytocin levels in both the dog and the owner. Adopt an animal, snuggle with a pet you already have, or offer to dog-sit for a friend if you have the opportunity.

Yes, you can hug yourself anytime you need one—oxytocin will still be released. Make it a habit to hug the ones you care for regularly. If you're comfortable doing so, have ended your relationship with your narcissistic partner, and can tell the difference between physical contact and emotional connection, you may want to spend time with someone you like—but only if you can see them as a casual partner—during this time, attempting to form a long-term relationship is discouraged until you feel ready.

Keep it simple—interact with, speak to, or go on a casual date with someone who has no strings attached if you can keep your expectations and investment modest. Be aware that engaging in sexual activity with this individual can tie you to them, so behave appropriately based on what you think you can handle, as this can be triggering and retraumatizing. We're not attempting to form a new bond with a potentially harmful partner; rather, we're allowing flirtation and social bonding.

This method would not work for everyone because not everyone can separate physical attraction from anything more sinister, but for others, going on a simple date or flirting with someone else will provide a pleasurable diversion and help the survivor feel like a loveable, attractive human being again. It will also inform you that, aside from the narcissist, you have other options for near touch and intimacy with other beings. I would only caution you against serial dating. It can lead to problems, rejection, and further abandonment if you get attached to a casual partner or multiple partners for some reason.

Boost Social Bonding

According to new findings, oxytocin can help people with PTSD symptoms have more compassion and pro-social behaviour (Palgi et al., 2016). Intimacy is at the heart of oxytocin bonding. While this type of bonding has been discussed in the context of intimate relationships, there's no reason to believe it doesn't work in other situations.

Hang out with friends who care about you to increase love, intimacy, and social ties in your life. Join a new gym or community group if you don't have any supportive mates. It will force you to engage with others. Because of the connection between oxytocin and compassion, it can be beneficial to support a friend, contribute to a cause, or lend someone a listening ear. You will not only motivate others, but you will also feel better. It's a win-win scenario for everyone involved.

It's also essential to practise self-compassion, as research suggests that this may boost oxytocin levels as well. Meditations on loving-kindness will help you develop compassion for yourself and others. See Dr Kristin Neff's Huffington Post article "The Chemicals of Care: How Self-Compassion Manifests in Our Bodies" for more detail on the connection between self-compassion and oxytocin.

Boost Dopamine and Adrenaline

I'm combining these two bad boys because I can fight them both with the same tactics. Are you looking for a shot of adrenaline? Take up a new hobby that makes you shiver with terror and excitement. Do things that offer you the thrill that the narcissist used to give you, whether it's rock climbing, skydiving, bungee jumping, or confidently going on a job interview. I guarantee it would be a better outcome than trying to get a thrill from a toxic relationship. Do you want to give your incentive scheme a boost?

Take up a new hobby, a new volunteer venture, or a new initiative with nothing to do with the narcissist to create new incentive circuits that have nothing to do with the narcissist. Consider the following scenario:

Pursue your interests and look for career openings that interest you. I started a YouTube channel, wrote a book, got a new job, and went to Meetups to meet new people during my No Contact journey. This reinforced my incentive system in a positive rather than negative way. It also gave me hope that I was rebuilding a better life with a new support system—hope is so important in moving on from the destruction of a toxic relationship. What are three things, ambitions, or hobbies you should be doing right now to replace the time and energy you wasted with the narcissist?

Make a fun bucket list, and instead of letting it sit around collecting dust, start doing the things on it. Make sure this list includes things that will both challenge and excite you, as well as an element of "fear" (healthy fear this time!) to make your upcoming schedule as volatile as your narcissist's hot and cold conduct. On my journey, for example, I had a range of experiences that made life more interesting and exciting, ranging from the bizarre and absurd to satisfying and challenging. Anything from my first time riding a mechanical bull to taking a pole dancing class (for the sole purpose of fitness, of course) to ride my first roller coaster. I also joined a brand new gym, attended an art therapy group, and took my first ever yoga class in a scalding hot room. Try things you've never done before, and do things you've done before in a different way—whether it's only for fun or for positive activity, the brain and body will thank you.

There's no limit to what you can do! Without the narcissist, life can be exciting and, yes, even more pleasurable. It's time to lavish all of the attention, enthusiasm, comfort, and self-care on yourself. Make sure you do these things on the spur of the moment and try new things. Every day, I used to look up various activities to see what new adventure I will be going on. Dopamine in your brain can circulate more freely due to this erratic, "intermittent" schedule of rewards. That sentence was written by me. I believe I've hit the pinnacle of nerddom.

Go out with people who make you feel good. These friends must be people who, without a doubt, make you happy because of their upbeat and welcoming attitudes. Friends who make you laugh, who always have a nice time with you, and who love you unconditionally will get the dopamine flowing like no other.

Plan solo dates with yourself instead, which will give you some "me" time while still offering enjoyment. Buying your favourite food, going to the gym, relaxing in a bubble bath with scented oils and candles, having a massage, purchasing a new wardrobe, purchasing a trip to a country you've always wanted to visit— whatever makes you happy, do it more often on your own at this time. This will make you become more self-reliant and less people-pleasing because you will realize the good experiences you had on your own and will be less likely to cling to negative people just to have them with you on any trip you go on.

Of course, wherever possible, strive to provide an element of surprise by adding something "different" to this solo date—food you haven't experienced, a place you haven't visited, or a country you haven't visited even if it's just to bed and breakfast in a different town or state, getaway for at least a weekend. This will provide you with a much-needed break, reminding you that your life will go on whether or not the narcissist is present.

Ease Up On Your Cortisol Levels

We'd rather not get any of this hormone in our bodies. Physical exercise, mindfulness, meditation, humour, music, and social networking are only a few of the forms suggested combating the hormone's effects.

So, when you're recovering, why not try a meditation or yoga class to lower these levels? Here are some suggestions:

- To reduce tension, attend a regular or weekly Vinyasa Flow yoga class and/or do a ten-minute breathing meditation every morning.
- If you want to tickle the funny bone, watch more comedy shows and movies. Laughter reduces cortisol levels, which feeds the reward system.
- Even if you don't want to, smile, smiling activates endorphins, which help you relax.
- Schedule a weekly night out with a few of your most encouraging friends to strengthen your social ties. Participate in an assault victim network or support group.
- Listen to music that reflects the various grief and rage stages that you can go through following an abusive relationship.

Pro-tips from a Self-Care Warrior: When you open your mouth slightly and let your tongue go limp, your brain stem and limbic system receive a signal to turn off cortisol and adrenaline. You can minimize cortisol levels by contracting your muscles and taking fast, rapid breaths for a quick pick-me-up. Isn't that cool?!

Detaching from the narcissist in your life needs relaxation and self-soothing. If you're thinking of reconnecting with your narcissistic spouse, they'll help you take a step back and fight your urges.

Serotonin Boost

When serotonin levels are poor, it can affect your impulsivity, ability to act on plans, feelings, memory, weight, sleep, and self-esteem. It can trigger ruminative addiction to your ex-partner. Try these natural serotonin boosters to enhance this strong hormone, some of which are discussed by Alex Korb, PhD (2011) in "Boosting Your Serotonin Activity."

- Sunlight—Sunlight exposure raises serotonin levels. To get your regular dose, go for morning and afternoon walks where it is likely sunny.
- B-vitamins—Serotonin deficiency can lead to depression. Vitamins B6 and B12 can help to reduce the risk of depression. According to Cornell Women's Health, a correlation has been discovered between low B6 and B12 levels and depression. B vitamins have also been discovered to be essential for the production of dopamine and serotonin.
- Massage—Research shows that massage therapy may help lower cortisol levels and increase serotonin and dopamine levels, particularly in vulnerable populations, including depressed pregnant mothers, cancer patients, and migraine sufferers (Field, 2005).
- Recalling happy memories—Remembering happy memories, according to Korb (2011), will increase serotonin output in the anterior cingulate cortex, a part of the brain that regulates attention. If you need help

visualizing happy memories, look through old photo albums, notes, and home videos. There is a dual effect as we recall happier memories: we increase serotonin while also stopping ourselves from ruminating on negative events.

Self-care warrior pro-tip: Don't use this technique to reminisce or romanticize about better times with your violent ex-partner. Create a regular thank list of items that made you happy that are unrelated to your ex-partner.

➢ **Therapy**—Talking to a mental health specialist who has dealt with narcissistic violence in both relationships and communities is another way to address these trauma ties. Someone well-versed and validated in this field will assist you in uncovering wounds under the surface that you might not be aware of. In the segment "Traditional Healing Methods Explained," I'll go through the various forms of therapy available.

➢ **Medications**—Medications such as SSRIs, for example, will help if you are suffering from serious, debilitating anxiety or depression. They are, however, outside the reach of this book's discussion. Often seek advice from a doctor or mental health professional on the right treatment for you. Never use any of these methods to "replace" the medicine you're taking; they're supposed to be a complement to your self-care routine, not a substitute for therapy. Any improvement in your current prescription should always be discussed with your mental health provider since side effects could.

➢ **Baby, get some exercise!**— If you're in an abusive relationship, hoping to quit, or have already begun the road to No Contact, any kind of exercise–whether treadmill running, weight lifting, dancing, yoga, walking, biking, or Zumba–acts as a natural antidepressant and helps you deal with your emotions more effectively at whatever stage of recovery you're in.

Pro-tip from the Self-Care Warrior: Many of these biochemicals can be targeted simultaneously by exercise. Jumping jacks, squats, and running in place all trigger a release of neurotransmitters such as norepinephrine, dopamine, and serotonin. Exercise can also help to reduce cortisol levels. If you don't already have a gym membership and a membership to your nearest yoga centre, I strongly advise you to do so.

CONCLUSION

In today's world, narcissism is affecting an increasing number of people. If narcissism was once an uncommon occurrence, it is now on a steady and dangerous increase. The social network that can be found everywhere on the Internet is what is causing this increase to be quicker than it should be.

It has massively improved the chances of encountering a narcissist. Prepare yourself for any obstacle he can throw your way. If you must live with a narcissist, it is critical that you take the necessary precautions to ensure your safety. Be ready for all of his angry outbursts.

Narcissists are master manipulators and can be incredibly charming. So be on the lookout for any ruse he can try to pull on you. Nowadays, it is very simple to develop a narcissistic personality. Taking a few selfies or making a few self-congratulatory remarks on social media isn't needed to turn you into a modern-day Narcissus. However, keeping such experiences to a bare minimum would be better for your own interests.

No one is going to look at your Facebook or Twitter profile to determine your worth. Maintain your emotional equilibrium. Don't let yourself get to the point where you don't care for anything but yourself. Indulging in luxuries can be a necessary part of certain people's lives. Often place a higher importance on people and relationships than on material possessions.

In the other side, you can both see a psychotherapist so that you have a safe place where you can talk through appropriate channels and in a secure environment. This is highly recommended because he would be compelled to listen in such a setting, and it may even work in your favor. If you want to love him despite his flaws and plan to spend the rest of your life with him, be very careful how you treat him. If you have any concerns or are unsure, you should strongly consider pursuing professional assistance. If a relationship consists of physical or emotional torment, it is no longer worth fighting for. Remove yourself from such people and start over.

It is not a crime to have narcissistic traits because they are always the product of circumstances beyond your control. Childhood experiences and their consequences play a significant role in defining a person's personality. If you put your heart and soul into it, it can be handled and you can heal to lead a perfectly normal life.

However, if you are on the other side of the divide, enduring abuse from narcissists, whether from a loved one, your lover, parent or even at work; I hope the information from this book is enough to guide you on how to protect yourself against emotional predators like narcissists described in this book. I hope you find your happy and safe haven soon. I wish you the best of luck on your path to a more positive mental state.

ABOUT THE AUTHOR

John Stam is an author and a life coach with over 10 years of experience in helping people through stress, depression, and other life crisis. His passion is in helping other live with purpose and more fulfilled. As a life coach, he has created a safe and comfortable environment that allows others to be themselves and express their views.

In his latest book, How to stop overthinking, he highlights steps towards self-acceptance, healing, and living life one day at a time. His aim is to heal the world by reaching as many people as possible. He hopes that through his book he can fulfill this dream. John attained a bachelor's degree in Psychology. This enables him to offer professional help to his clients.

During his leisure time, you will find John spending time with his family, reading books, and experiencing new cultures. With his unique charm and friendly personality, John easily bonds with others and has made many friends all over the world.

Dear Reader,

Thanks for reading "NARCISSISTS step by step guide to deal with narcissism in your relationship , in family and in your workplace". I'd appreciate it if you leave a review for this story. It goes a long way to help my author business. Thank you!

If you liked this book you can follow me on amazon.com "John Stam" and be the first to see my new books.

https://www.amazon.com/~/e/B08WL3QW9G

Let's connect

John101stam@gmail.com

Printed in Great Britain
by Amazon